ISBN 978-0-243-25488-0
PIBN 10790519

1 MONTH OF
FREE
READING

at

www.ForgottenBooks.com

By purchasing this book you are eligible for one month membership to ForgottenBooks.com, giving you unlimited access to our entire collection of over 700,000 titles via our web site and mobile apps.

To claim your free month visit:

www.forgottenbooks.com/free790519

English
Français
Deutsche
Italiano
Español
Português

www.forgottenbooks.com

Mythology Photography **Fiction**
Fishing Christianity **Art** Cooking
Essays Buddhism Freemasonry
Medicine **Biology** Music **Ancient Egypt** Evolution Carpentry Physics
Dance Geology **Mathematics** Fitness
Shakespeare **Folklore** Yoga Marketing
Confidence Immortality Biographies
Poetry **Psychology** Witchcraft
Electronics Chemistry History **Law**
Accounting **Philosophy** Anthropology
Alchemy Drama Quantum Mechanics
Atheism Sexual Health **Ancient History**
Entrepreneurship Languages Sport
Paleontology Needlework Islam
Metaphysics Investment Archaeology
Parenting Statistics Criminology
Motivational

SAILOR'S COMPANION,

OR

BOOK OF DEVOTIONS FOR SEAMEN

IN PUBLIC AND PRIVATE.

PHILADELPHIA:
PRESBYTERIAN BOARD OF PUBLICATION.
NO. 821 CHESTNUT STREET.

INTRODUCTION.

THE volume here presented to Mariners was prepared expressly for their use. The First Part is designed for public services on ship-board, while the Second Part is intended chiefly for private use. The vocation of a sailor is both useful and honourable; and could a religious feeling be more generally infused into these brave and enduring men, not only would their own happiness be promoted, but additional respect would be entertained for their profession. A book for their especial benefit has been long desired, and the present may answer a good purpose, until a better one supplies its place. By the serious and devout use of it, under the divine blessing, it is hoped that the seamen in the naval service of the United States and in the commercial marine, to whom it is hereby dedicated, may receive lasting advantage.

Nothing sectarian will be found in these pages.

CONTENTS.

PART FIRST,

PUBLIC SERVICES.

PLAIN AND SHORT DISCOURSES ON THE PRINCIPAL DOCTRINES OF THE GOSPEL.

CONTENTS.

PART SECOND,

FOR MORE PRIVATE USE.

PUBLIC SERVICES.

FORM OF SERVICE

ON

SHIP-BOARD ON THE LORD'S DAY.

THE SHIP'S COMPANY BEING REVERENTLY ASSEMBLED, SOME SUITABLE PERSON WILL CONDUCT THE WORSHIP IN THE FOLLOWING ORDER.

These Scriptures to be deliberately read.

O COME, let us worship and bow down; let us kneel before the Lord our maker.

The sacrifices of God are a broken spirit; a broken and contrite heart, O God, thou wilt not despise.

The eyes of the Lord are upon the righteous, and his ears are open to their cry.

He that cometh to God must believe that he is, and that he is a rewarder of them that diligently seek him.

Let us come boldly to the throne of grace, that we may obtain mercy and find grace to help in time of need.

Then follows the Introductory Prayer.

ALMIGHTY God, our heavenly Father, thy throne is in the heavens, and thy government extends over the land and the sea. In thy mercy and condescension thou dost permit us to approach

(7)

and make our common supplications to thee. Fulfil to us at this time thy gracious promise, that where two or three are met together in thy name, thou wilt be in the midst of them. May a sense of thy excellency make us suitably afraid, and may no vain and sinful thoughts lodge within us. Give to us the spirit of true worshippers, and may we not mock thee with a mere outward form of devotion in which our hearts are not engaged. May we pray to thee in all sincerity, joyfully celebrate thy praise, and reverently hear thy most holy word. Hear thou the voice of our supplication; cleanse us from every sin, and accept of us and our services for the sake of Jesus Christ, to whom with thee and the Holy Spirit, be endless praises, Amen.

Or this ·

O MOST holy God, to whom all worship is due, give to us the aids of thy Spirit, that we may worship thee aright. May we at this time be solemn and devout, and withdraw our thoughts from the business and cares of the world. Suffer no temptation to assail us by which our attention might be diverted from the duty in which we are engaged; but impart to us thy grace and strength, that we may penitently confess our sins, and exercise faith in the Lamb of God, who taketh away the sins of the world; all which we ask for Jesus Christ's sake, Amen.

Here read one of the Selections from Scripture, which may be found under the head of SCRIPTURE SELECTIONS.

Then one of the Psalms or Hymns at the end of the Book may be read or sung.

Then some of the following Prayers, or any of those under the head of "Prayers for various occasions," are to be devoutly repeated.

Confession of sin.

O MOST holy God, thou art of purer eyes than to look upon sin without displeasure; and yet we have been sinners from our youth, until our iniquities are more in number than the hairs of our head. Thy most holy commandments we have broken, notwithstanding the danger to which our souls have thereby been exposed. Our affections have been earthly and sensual, our lips have uttered vanity and profaned thy holy name, and all our members have been made instruments of unrighteousness. These our sins we would not vainly attempt to conceal from thee; but penitently confessing them, we would implore thee for pardon, and for strength to live a new life, for the sake of Jesus Christ, Amen.

A Prayer for Divine Guidance.

O LORD most merciful, from whom all good purposes do proceed, grant unto us heavenly wisdom to direct our steps aright, that we may be obedient to all lawful authority, and faithfully perform all our duties. Thou hast required of us, in whatever situation we may be placed, to adorn it by a holy walk, and to remember that thine eyes are continually upon us. May the example of our blessed Redeemer be ever before us, and may we strive to follow in his footsteps, so that when we shall depart from this life we may hear thee say, Well done, good and faithful servants, enter ye into the joy of the Lord; which we ask for Christ's sake, Amen.

A Prayer for Protection.

O ALMIGHTY God, who rulest the sea, and according to thy good pleasure, makest it a dangerous or safe highway, hold us in thy hand that no evil may befall us. In our helplessness and insignificance, we need the protection of more than a mortal power. Send us, we beseech thee, favouring winds that we may be speeded on our voyage; and may we be preserved from fire, tempest, shipwreck, and the other dangers of the deep. May our life and health be precious in thy sight, that in safety we may reach our destined port, which we ask for Christ's sake, Amen.

A Prayer for Friends.

O GOD, in thee all live and have their being, and to thee are we indebted for all the blessings of home and friends. In our absence, may those who are near and dear to us be under thy holy protection, and be kept in life and health. May they not be led into temptation, neither let temporal or spiritual evil befall them. Fathers and mothers, wives and children, brothers and sisters, we would keep in our affectionate remembrance; and we would earnestly beseech thee to keep them in thy remembrance, for thy favour is life, and thy loving-kindness is better than life. All which we ask for Christ's sake, Amen.

A Prayer for sick Messmates.

O THOU to whom we are indebted for life and health and all things, to thee alone we would repair when sickness befalls us or our companions. In thy wise dispensations thou hast seen fit to send sickness among us; and by thy mercy alone can it be removed. Thou art the great Physician, and without thy blessing all human skill will be in vain. Apply then thy healing aid that our companions may be restored to health, or if, in thy wisdom, thou hast determined that in any case the sickness should terminate in death, then mercifully prepare the dying for their departure, and through the merits of Christ's sacrifice introduce their spirits into that world where there shall be no more sickness nor death; and to thy name, Father, Son, and Holy Ghost, shall be all the glory, Amen.

A Prayer for our beloved Country.

O MOST merciful God, thou hast made us citizens of a favoured land, and hast given us a goodly heritage. For good and wholesome laws we thank thee, by which life, liberty, and personal rights are protected. May our country ever be under thy holy care, and by thy almighty power preserve it from civil dissension and foreign invasion. Let no weapon prosper which is raised against it, and may its blessed institutions be perpetuated to remote ages. Ward off famine, pestilence, and every deadly evil; may its people lead industrious, peaceable, and godly lives; and may all its officers, from the highest to the lowest, be imbued with heavenly wisdom, and be a terror to evil doers, while they are a praise to them that do well; which we ask for Christ's sake, Amen.

A Prayer for general good Conduct.

O LORD, it is not in man to direct his steps, and without thy grace we will err and stray from the path in which we should go. Give to us, we pray thee, the disposition to do right in all circumstances. May we neither tempt others to sin, nor be tempted by them. May we be attentive to duty; respectful to those in command over us; friendly to one another; courageous and firm in times of danger; and humble before our God. Guard our hearts from passion; our lips from profanity; and our hands from fraud and dishonesty. May an ever present sense of our obligation to thee preserve us, in foreign ports, from

extravagance, intemperance, profanity, and licentiousness; and do thou graciously guard us from
the numerous temptations which may beset us;
and from the arts and enticements of the wicked,
who may wish us to do evil. All which we ask
for Jesus Christ's sake, Amen.

The Lord's Prayer.

OUR Father which art in heaven, hallowed be thy
name; thy kingdom come; thy will be done in earth
as it is in heaven; give us this day our daily bread; and
forgive us our debts as we forgive our debtors; and lead
us not into temptation, but deliver us from evil; for thine
is the kingdom, and the power, and the glory, for ever,
Amen.

Here one of the Sermons in another part of the Book is to be
read.

Then close with this Prayer.

LORD, accept our feeble attempts to worship
thee, and may a solemn influence abide with
us from the services in which we have been engaged. Impress the truth which we have heard
upon our hearts; and may we not only endeavour
to learn the will of God, but put it into practice
in our lives. Forgive all that thou hast seen amiss
in us at this time, and accept of our persons and
services for Christ's sake, Amen.

Glory be to the Father, and to the Son, and to the
Holy Ghost; as it was in the beginning, is now,
and ever shall be, world without end, Amen.

2

A SECOND FORM FOR PUBLIC WORSHIP.

These Scriptures should be devoutly read.

THE Lord your God is God of gods, and Lord of lords, a great God, a mighty, and a terrible, which regardeth not persons, nor taketh reward

Thine, O Lord, is the greatness, and the power, and the glory, and the victory, and the majesty; for all that is in the heaven, and in the earth, is thine; thine is the kingdom, O Lord, and thou art exalted as head above all.

Though the Lord be high, yet hath he respect unto the lowly; but the proud he knoweth afar off.

The darkness hideth not from thee, but the night shineth as the day; the darkness and the light are both alike to thee.

O Lord, thou hast searched me and known me. Thou knowest my down-sitting and mine up-rising, thou understandest my thoughts afar off. Thou compassest my path and my lying down, and art acquainted with all my ways. For there is not a word in my tongue, but lo, O Lord, thou knowest it altogether.

He is wise in heart and mighty in strength: who hath hardened himself against him, and hath prospered?

Wherefore we receiving a kingdom that cannot be moved, let us have grace, whereby we may serve God acceptably, with reverence and godly fear

Introductory Prayer.

O GOD most holy, thou art the infinite Spirit, and they that would worship thee, must worship thee in spirit and in truth. So govern our thoughts and regulate our affections, that we may present thee an acceptable sacrifice, with which thou wilt be well pleased. May our duty to thee be our pleasure; and with the angels in heaven, and the spirits of the just made perfect, may we joyfully ascribe all glory to the Most High. May thy presence be with us, and thy grace assist us that we may not mock thee with mere lip-service, in which our hearts are not found. Teach us all good knowledge, and scatter darkness from our minds. For the sake of thy well-beloved Son, our Saviour, may the words of our mouth, and the meditations of our hearts be acceptable in thy sight, O Lord, our Strength and our Redeemer, Amen.

Or this :

O LORD, our Creator, Redeemer, and Friend, we would, with one accord, acknowledge thee in thy works of majesty and power; in the redemption which thou hast wrought by the sufferings and death of Jesus Christ; and in all the dispensations of thy gracious providence. We would come and worship before thee, in the full assurance that thou wilt hear the prayers of the humble, and bestow on us the things which we need. May we ask that we may receive; seek that we may find; and knock that the door of mercy may be opened. Keep us from wandering thoughts and desires, that the services in which we are engaged may do us good, as they do the upright in heart. All which we ask for Jesus Christ's sake, Amen.

Here read one of the Selections from Scripture, which may be found under the head of Scripture Selections.

Then one of the Psalms or Hymns at the end of the Book may be read or sung.

Then some of the following Prayers are to be devoutly repeated.

A general Confession.

ALMIGHTY and most merciful Father, we have erred and strayed from thy ways like lost sheep. We have followed too much the devices and desires of our own hearts. We have offended against thy holy laws. We have left undone those things which we ought to have done; and we have done those things which we ought not to have done; and there is no health in us. But thou, O Lord, have mercy upon us, miserable offenders. Spare thou those, O God, who confess their faults. Restore thou those who are penitent, according to thy promises declared unto mankind, in Christ Jesus our Lord; and grant, O most merciful Father, for his sake, that we may hereafter live a godly, righteous, and sober life, to the glory of thy holy name, Amen.

A Prayer for Repentance and Faith.

O GOD, from whom all gracious affections do proceed, grant unto us such an insight into our hearts as will thoroughly convince us of our native depravity, and numberless actual transgressions. May we not vainly attempt to excuse or cloak our sins, which are fully exposed to thy all-seeing eye; but humbly confess them, truly repent of them, and heartily forsake them, that we may thereby obtain thy great mercy in the forgiveness of the same, according to thy promise, that whoso confesseth and forsaketh his sins shall have mercy. And grant, we beseech thee, that faith in Jesus Christ, by which we shall be enabled to look to him, and trust in him as the only Saviour of them that are lost. May we look to him as God manifested in the flesh, and may we flee to his cross, on which he suffered, the just for the unjust, that he might bring us to God. May we not be faithless, but believing; may we not depend on any merit of our own, but cast our souls on Him who hath said, Him that cometh to me I will in no wise cast out; and this we ask for Jesus Christ's sake, Amen

A Prayer for Christian Tempers.

O GOD, who searchest the heart, and requirest that it should be right in thy sight, create in us a clean heart, and renew a right spirit within us, that we may be renewed and sanctified and made meet for the Master's service. Thou, O Lord, knowest that we cannot control our thoughts and tempers, without thy special grace. We are prone to sin as the sparks fly upwards; and, like the restless sea, are tossed to and fro by our un-

2 *

governed passions. Send thou thy Holy Spirit to breathe into us a new life, and deliver us from our old corruptions. May anger, malice, envy, evil speaking, and lust, be suppressed; and may we hereafter be characterized by love, joy, peace, long-suffering, gentleness, goodness, faith, meekness, and temperance, which are so well pleasing in thy sight. May the same mind and temper which dwelt in Christ Jesus dwell in us; which we ask for his sake, Amen.

A Prayer for God's Care.

THOU, Lord, not only hast all power, but art everywhere present. Thou gatherest the waters of the sea together as a heap, and layest up the depth in store-houses. Thy way is in the whirl-wind and in the storm, and the clouds are the dust of thy feet. O most mighty God, cast the shield of thy protection around us, who go down to the sea in ships, and do business in great waters, and who see the works of the Lord and his wonders in the deep. When thou dost command and raise the stormy wind, and lift up the waves thereof, may we cry to thee in our trouble, who makest the storm a calm, so that the waves thereof are still. Preserve us from shipwreck, accidents, and sudden death, and in thy hands may we ever be safe. Hitherto thou hast been our help amidst a thousand dangers. Withhold not thou thy mercy from us for the future ; which we ask for Christ's sake, Amen.

A Prayer for a religious Frame of mind.

O LORD most holy, thou requirest in us a constant conformity to thee, not only in our outward conduct, but in the thoughts and intents of our hearts; and yet how sadly do we fall short! Our thoughts, even when we are assembled for thy worship, often wander with the fool's eyes to the ends of the earth; while our goodness is as the morning cloud and early dew which passeth away. O Lord, inspire us with a better and holier disposition of mind. May we regard thee with reverence and godly fear, and at all times remember that thou, God, seest us. Help us ever to preserve a devout frame of mind; and in the midst of our worldly occupations, as well as in the hours of public worship, may our affections be raised from earth to heaven, and our meditations be of God and heavenly things. As we know not what an hour may bring forth, teach us, at all times, to be in that state of mind in which we should wish to be found, when our Lord shall call us hence; and the praise shall be to the Father, the Son, and the Holy Ghost, Amen.

A Prayer for a true, religious Hope.

OUR heavenly Father, who, in thy infinite mercy, didst send thy beloved Son into the world to seek and save the lost, inspire us with that good hope which shall not fail us in the end. May it not be the hope of the hypocrite, which shall perish; or that delusive hope of the wicked, which is built on the sand; but that blessed expectation, which is founded on the sacrifice and intercession of our Redeemer. Give to us the hope that will purify our hearts, raise our thoughts above the world, and shed a holy light upon our dying hour. We dare not hope that thou wilt accept us for any righteousness which we may have done, for our best works are not sufficient to satisfy the just claims of thy law. Our expectation is from the Redeemer, who died and rose again for our justification. Graciously dismiss our fears; scatter the clouds which darken our minds; and when we come to die, may we have that blessed hope, that we shall die in the Lord and be for ever with him; which we ask alone for his sake, Amen.

Here one of the brief Sermons is to be deliberately and seriously read.

Concluding Prayer.

O HOLY and most gracious God, may the words of thy truth, which we have heard with our outward ears, be engrafted inwardly upon our hearts. Like seed sown upon good ground, may it bring forth its fruit in due season. May we give the more earnest heed to the things which we have heard, lest at any time we should let them slip. In all our services, may thy great name be glorified, and our own souls enlightened and saved; which we ask for Christ s sake, Amen.

Benediction.

The Lord Jesus Christ be with your spirits. Grace be with you, Amen.

FUNERAL SERVICE

TO BE USED AT SEA.

THE BODY BEING DULY PREPARED FOR BURIAL, AND THE SHIP'S
COMPANY BEING ASSEMBLED, THE PERSON OFFICIATING SHALL
SAY

WHAT is your life? It is is even a vapour that appeareth for a little time and then vanisheth away.
My days are swifter than a weaver's shuttle, swifter than a post they flee away. They are passed away as the swift ships; as the eagle that hasteth to the prey.

We brought nothing into this world, and it is certain, we can carry nothing out. The Lord gave, and the Lord hath taken away, blessed be the name of the Lord.

What man is he that liveth and shall not see death? Shall he deliver his soul from the hand of the grave?

There is an appointed time for man upon earth; his days are as the days of an hireling; his days are determined, the number of his months is with thee; thou hast appointed his bounds that he cannot pass.

Then shall be used the following prayer.

O HOLY and righteous Governor of the world it is by thy good pleasure that we live, and when thou commandest, our countenances are changed, and we are sent away. Make thou us to know our end, and the measure of our days, what it is, that we may know how frail we are.

(22)

As it has pleased thee, O Lord, to send the messenger of death among us, and to recall the spirit of one of our number, we beseech thee that we may lay it to heart, and remember that we also are mortal; knowing neither the day nor the hour in which our summons may come. Grant that by a wise care of piety, we may be prepared to meet thee in the judgment; and by living a godly, righteous, and sober life, be ready to go hence in joy, and not in fear. Cheer thou us with the assurance, that although the wages of sin is death, yet the gift of God is eternal life, through Jesus Christ our Lord, Amen.

Hear now the admonitory and comfortable words of Holy Scripture.

LORD, thou hast been our dwelling place in all generations. Before the mountains were brought forth, or ever thou hadst formed the earth and the world, even from everlasting to everlasting, thou art God. Thou turnest man to destruction, and sayest: Return, ye children of men. For a thousand years in thy sight are but as yesterday when it is past, and as a watch in the night. Thou carriest them away as with a flood; they are as a sleep; in the morning they are like grass which groweth up. In the morning it flourisheth and groweth up; in the evening it is cut down and withereth. For we are consumed by thine anger, and by thy wrath are we troubled. Thou hast set our iniquities before thee, our secret sins in the light of thy countenance. For all our days are passed away in thy wrath; we spend our years as a tale that is told. The days of our years are threescore years and ten; and if by reason of strength they be fourscore years, yet is their strength labour and sorrow; for it is soon cut off and we fly away. So teach us to number our days, that we may apply our hearts unto wisdom.

Verily, verily, I say unto you, he that heareth my word and believeth on him that sent me, hath everlasting life, and shall not come into condemnation; but is passed from death unto life. Verily, verily, I say unto you, The hour is coming, and now is, when the dead shall hear the voice of the Son of God; and they that hear shall live. Marvel not at this, for the hour is coming in the which all that are in the graves shall hear his voice and shall come forth; they that have done good, unto the resurrection of life; and they that have done evil, unto the resurrection of damnation.

Jesus said, I am the resurrection and the life; he that believeth on me, though he were dead, yet shall he live; and whosoever liveth and believeth on me shall never die.

For this corruptible must put on incorruption, and this mortal must put on immortality. So when this corruptible shall have put on incorruption, and this mortal shall have put on immortality, then shall be brought to pass the saying that is written, Death is swallowed up in victory. O death, where is thy sting? O grave, where is thy victory? The sting of death is sin, and the strength of sin is the law. But thanks be to God who giveth us the victory through our Lord Jesus Christ.

Then all being ready for the burial, the person officiating shall say:

FORASMUCH as it hath pleased Almighty God to remove out of this world the soul of this our late companion, we do now commit his lifeless body to the bosom of the mighty deep, [Here the body is to be committed to the sea,]* in the full

---

* If the funeral shall take place in port, say, "We do now commit his lifeless body to the earth whence it was taken."

persuasion, that it shall be raised again, in the resurrection of the last day, when the dead shall come forth from their graves, and when the sea shall give up its dead.

Concluding Prayer.

O GOD, who ever livest and abidest, may we all be made duly sensible of the shortness and uncertainty of life. We are but dust, and unto dust we shall return; but thou dost give us an endless life, which shall survive the destruction of all these material things. May we in faith and hope await our appointed time till our change shall come; and when the earthly house of this tabernacle is dissolved, may we have a building of God, an house not made with hands, eternal in the heavens. And do thou, O most compassionate God, impart thy blessing to the surviving friends of the deceased, that when they learn that they are to see his face no more, they may find in Jesus a sympathizing friend who sticketh closer than a brother. Send now to them and to us thy salvation; and wash us in the atoning blood of Him, who died upon the cross; that whether we live, we may live unto the Lord, or whether we die, we may die unto the Lord; so that whether we live or die, we may be the Lord's. All which we ask for Jesus Christ's sake, Amen.

The grace of our Lord Jesus Christ, and the love of God, and the fellowship of the Holy Ghost, be with us all for evermore, Amen.

3

SCRIPTURE SELECTIONS.

SELECTION I.

Hear the word of God as recorded in the twenty-fourth Psalm.

THE earth is the LORD's, and the fulness thereof; the world, and they that dwell therein:

For he hath founded it upon the seas, and established it upon the floods.

Who shall ascend into the hill of the LORD? or who shall stand in his holy place?

He that hath clean hands, and a pure heart; who hath not lifted up his soul unto vanity, nor sworn deceitfully.

He shall receive the blessing from the Lord, and righteousness from the God of his salvation.

This is the generation of them that seek him, that seek thy face, O Jacob. Selah.

Lift up your heads, O ye gates; and be ye lift up, ye everlasting doors; and the King of glory shall come in.

Who is this King of glory? The LORD strong and mighty, the LORD mighty in battle.

Lift up your heads, O ye gates; even lift them up, ye everlasting doors; and the King of glory shall come in.

Who is this King of glory? The LORD of hosts, he is the King of glory. Selah.

(26)

Hear again the word of God as recorded in the sixth chapter of Matthew.

NO man can serve two masters : for either he will hate the one, and love the other ; or else he will hold to the one, and despise the other.   Ye cannot serve God and Mammon.   Therefore I say unto you, Take no thought for your life, what ye shall eat, or what ye shall drink ; nor yet for your body, what ye shall put on.   Is not the life more than meat, and the body than raiment ? Behold the fowls of the air : for they sow not, neither do they reap, nor gather into barns ; yet your heavenly Father feedeth them.   Are ye not much better than they ? Which of you by taking thought can add one cubit unto his stature ?   And why take ye thought for raiment ? Consider the lilies of the field, how they grow ; they toil not, neither do they spin : and yet I say unto you, that even Solomon in all his glory was not arrayed like one of these.   Wherefore if God so clothe the grass of the field, which to-day is, and to-morrow is cast into the oven, shall he not much more clothe you, O ye of little faith ? Therefore take no thought, saying, What shall we eat ? or, What shall we drink ? or, Wherewithal shall we be clothed ?   (For after all these things do the Gentiles seek :) for your heavenly Father knoweth that ye have need of all these things.   But seek ye first the kingdom of God, and his righteousness ; and all these things shall be added unto you.   Take therefore no thought for the morrow : for the morrow shall take thought for the things of itself.   Sufficient unto the day is the evil thereof.

SELECTION II.

Hear the word of God as recorded in the first chapter of Isaiah.

WASH you, make you clean ; put away the evil of your doings from before mine eyes ; cease to do evil ; learn to do well : seek judgment, relieve the oppressed ; judge the fatherless ; plead for the widow. Come now, and let us reason together, saith the Lord :

though your sins be as scarlet, they shall be as white as snow ; though they be red like crimson, they shall be as wool.   If ye be willing and obedient, ye shall eat the good of the land : but if ye refuse and rebel, ye shall be devoured with the sword : for the mouth of the Lord hath spoken it.   How is the faithful city become a harlot ! It was full of judgment; righteousness lodged in it; but now murderers.   Thy silver has become dross, thy wine mixed with water.   Thy princes are rebellious, and companions of thieves : every one loveth gifts, and followeth after rewards : they judge not the fatherless, neither doth the cause of the widow come unto them.   Therefore saith the Lord, the Lord of hosts, the mighty One of Israel, Ah, I will ease me of mine adversaries, and avenge me of mine enemies : and I will turn my hand upon thee, and purely purge away thy dross, and take away all thy tin.   And I will restore thy judges as at the first, and thy counsellors as at the beginning : afterward thou shalt be called, The city of righteousness, The faithful city.   Zion shall be redeemed with judgment, and her converts with righteousness.

Hear again the word of God as recorded in the first chapter of the First Epistle of John.

THAT which was from the beginning, which we have heard, which we have seen with our eyes, which we have looked upon, and our hands have handled, of the Word of life, (for the Life was manifested, and we have seen it, and bear witness, and shew unto you that eternal Life, which was with the Father, and was manifested unto us ;) that which we have seen and heard declare we unto you, that ye also may have fellowship with us : and truly our fellowship is with the Father, and with his Son Jesus Christ.   And these things write we unto you, that your joy may be full.   This then is the message which we have heard of him, and declare unto you, that God is light, and in him is no darkness at all.   If we say that we have fellowship with him, and walk in darkness, we lie, and do not the truth : but if we walk in the light, as he is in the light, we have fellowship one with another, and the blood of Jesus Christ his Son cleanseth us from all sin. If we say that we have no sin, we deceive ourselves, and the truth is not in us. If we confess our sins, he is faithful and just to forgive us our sins, and to cleanse us from all unrighteousness. If we say that we have not sinned, we make him a liar, and his word is not in us.

SELECTION III.

Hear the word of God as recorded in the fifty-fifth chapter of Isaiah.

HO, every one that thirsteth, come ye to the waters, and he that hath no money ; come ye, buy, and eat ; yea, come, buy wine and milk without money and without price. Wherefore do ye spend money for that which is not bread ? and your labour for that which satisfieth not ? Hearken diligently unto me, and eat ye that which is good, and let your soul delight itself in fatness. Incline your ear, and come unto me : hear, and your soul shall live ; and I will make an everlasting covenant with you, even the sure mercies of David. Behold, I have given him for a witness to the people, a leader and commander to the people. Behold, thou shalt call a nation that thou knowest not, and nations that knew not thee shall run unto thee, because of the Lord thy God, and for the Holy One of Israel ; for he hath glorified thee. Seek ye the Lord while he may be found, call ye upon while he is near. Let the wicked forsake his way, and the unrighteous man his thoughts : and let him return unto the Lord, and he will have mercy upon him ; and to our God, for he will abundantly pardon.

For my thoughts are not your thoughts, neither are your ways my ways, saith the Lord. For as the heavens are higher than the earth, so are my ways higher than your ways, and my thoughts than your thoughts. For as

3 *

the rain cometh down, and the snow from heaven, and returneth not thither, but watereth the earth, and maketh it bring forth and bud, that it may give seed to the sower, and bread to the eater: so shall my word be that goeth forth out of my mouth: it shall not return unto me void, but it shall accomplish that which I please, and it shall prosper in the thing whereto I sent it.   For ye shall go out with joy, and be led forth with peace: the mountains and the hills shall break forth before you into singing, and all the trees of the field shall clap their hands.   Instead of the thorn shall come up the fir-tree, and instead of the brier shall come up the myrtle-tree: and it shall be to the Lord for a name, and for an everlasting sign that shall not be cut off.

Hear again the word of God as recorded in the eleventh chapter of Matthew.

AT that time Jesus answered and said, I thank thee, O Father, Lord of heaven and earth, because thou hast hid these things from the wise and prudent, and hast revealed them unto babes.   Even so, Father, for so it seemed good in thy sight.   All things are delivered unto me of my Father; and no man knoweth the Son, but the Father, neither knoweth any man the Father, save the Son, and he to whomsoever the Son will reveal him.

Come unto me, all ye that labour, and are heavy laden, and I will give you rest.   Take my yoke upon you, and learn of me: for I am meek and lowly in heart; and ye shall find rest unto your souls.   For my yoke is easy, and my burden is light.

SELECTION IV.

Hear the word of God as recorded in the one hundred and eleventh Psalm.

PRAISE ye the Lord.   I will praise the Lord with my whole heart, in the assembly of the upright, and in the congregation.   The works of the Lord are great, sought out of all them that have pleasure therein. His work is honourable and glorious: and his righteousness endureth for ever. He hath made his wonderful works to be remembered: the Lord is gracious and full of compassion. He hath given meat unto them that fear him: he will ever be mindful of his covenant. He hath shewed his people the power of his works, that he may give them the heritage of the heathen. The works of his hands are verity and judgment; all his commandments are sure. They stand fast for ever and ever, and are done in truth and uprightness. He sent redemption unto his people: he hath commanded his covenant for ever: holy and reverend is his name. The fear of the Lord is the beginning of wisdom: a good understanding have all they that do his commandments: his praise endureth for ever.

Hear again the word of God as recorded in the second chapter of Philippians.

IF there be therefore any consolation in Christ, if any comfort of love, if any fellowship of the Spirit, if any bowels and mercies, fulfil ye my joy, that ye be likeminded, having the same love, being of one accord, of one mind. Let nothing be done through strife or vain glory; but in lowliness of mind let each esteem other better than themselves. Look not every man on his own things, but every man also on the things of others. Let this mind be in you, which was also in Christ Jesus: Who, being in the form of God, thought it not robbery to be equal with God: but made himself of no reputation, and took upon him the form of a servant, and was made in the likeness of men: and being found in fashion as a man, he humbled himself, and became obedient unto death, even the death of the cross. Wherefore God also hath highly exalted him, and given him a name which is above every name: that at the name of Jesus every knee should bow, of things in heaven, and things in earth, and things under the earth; and that every tongue should confess that Jesus Christ is Lord, to the

glory of God the Father.   Wherefore, my beloved, as ye
have always obeyed, not as in my presence only, but now
much more in my absence, work out your own salvation
with fear and trembling.   For it is God which worketh
in you both to will and to do of his good pleasure.   Do
all things without murmurings and disputings : that ye
may be blameless and harmless, the sons of God, without
rebuke, in the midst of a crooked and perverse nation,
among whom ye shine as lights in the world.

SELECTION V.

Hear the word of God as recorded in the third chapter of Lam-
entations.

IT is of the Lord's mercies that we are not consumed,
because his compassions fail not.   They are new every
morning : great is thy faithfulness.   The Lord is my
portion, saith my soul; therefore will I hope in him.
The Lord is good unto them that wait for him, to the
soul that seeketh him.   It is good that a man should
both hope and quietly wait for the salvation of the Lord.
It is good for a man that he bear the yoke in his youth.
He sitteth alone, and keepeth silence, because he hath
borne it upon him.   He putteth his mouth in the dust;
if so be there may be hope.   He giveth his cheek to him
that smiteth him : he is filled full with reproach.   For
the Lord will not cast off for ever : but though he
cause grief, yet will he have compassion according to the
multitude of his mercies.   For he doth not afflict will-
ingly, nor grieve the children of men.   To crush under
his feet all the prisoners of the earth ; to turn aside the
right of a man before the face of the Most High ; to
subvert a man in his cause, the Lord approveth not.
Who is he that saith, and it cometh to pass, when the
Lord commandeth it not?   Out of the mouth of the
Most High proceedeth not evil and good?   Wherefore
doth a living man complain, a man for the punishment
of his sins?   Let us search and try our ways, and turn

again to the Lord. Let us lift up our heart with our hands unto God in the heavens.

Hear again the word of God as recorded in the tenth chapter of John.

THEN said Jesus unto them again, Verily, verily, I say unto you, I am the door of the sheep. All that ever came before me are thieves and robbers : but the sheep did not hear them. I am the door : by me if any man enter in, he shall be saved, and shall go in and out, and find pasture. The thief cometh not but for to steal, and to kill, and to destroy : I am come that they might have life, and that they might have it more abundantly. I am the good shepherd : the good shepherd giveth his life for the sheep. But he that is an hireling, and not the shepherd, whose own the sheep are not, seeth the wolf coming, and leaveth the sheep and fleeth : and the wolf catcheth them, and scattereth the sheep. The hireling fleeth, because he is an hireling, and careth not for the sheep. I am the good shepherd, and know my sheep, and am known of mine. As the Father knoweth me, even so know I the Father : and I lay down my life for the sheep. And other sheep I have, which are not of this fold : them also I must bring, and they shall hear my voice : and there shall be one fold, and one shepherd. Therefore doth my Father love me, because I lay down my life, that I might take it again. No man taketh it from me, but I lay it down of myself : I have power to lay it down, and I have power to take it again. This commandment have I received of my Father.

SELECTION VI.

Hear the word of God as recorded in the eighteenth chapter of Ezekiel.

THE soul that sinneth, it shall die. The son shall not bear the iniquity of the father, neither shall the father bear the iniquity of the son ; the righteousness of the righteous shall be upon him, and the wickedness of the wicked shall be upon him. But if the wicked will turn from all his sins that he hath committed, and keep all my statutes, and do that which is lawful and right, he shall surely live, he shall not die. All his transgressions that he hath committed, they shall not be mentioned unto him : in his righteousness that he hath done he shall live. Have I any pleasure at all that the wicked should die? saith the Lord God ; and not that he should return from his ways, and live? But when the righteous turneth away from his righteousness; and committeth iniquity, and doeth according to all the abominations that the wicked man doeth, shall he live? All his righteousness that he hath done shall not be mentioned : in his trespass that he hath trespassed, and in his sin that he hath sinned, in them shall he die. Yet ye say, The way of the Lord is not equal. Hear now, O house of Israel, is not my way equal? are not your ways unequal? When a righteous man turneth away from his righteousness, and committeth iniquity, and dieth in them, for his iniquity that he hath done, shall he die. Again, when the wicked man turneth away from his wickedness that he hath committed, and doeth that which is lawful and right, he shall save his soul alive. Because he considereth, and turneth away from all his transgressions that he hath committed, he shall surely live, he shall not die.

Hear again the word of God as recorded in the seventh chapter of Matthew.

ASK, and it shall be given you; seek, and ye shall find ; knock, and it shall be opened unto you. For every one that asketh, receiveth ; and he that seeketh, findeth ; and to him that knocketh, it shall be opened. Or what man is there of you, whom if his son ask bread, will he give him a stone? Or if he ask a fish, will he give him a serpent? If ye then, being evil, know how to give good gifts unto your children, how much more shall your Father which is in heaven give good things to them that ask him ? Therefore all things whatsoever ye would that men should do to you, do ye even so to them : for this is the law and the prophets.

Enter ye in at the strait gate : for wide is the gate, and broad is the way, that leadeth to destruction, and many there be which go in thereat : because strait is the gate, and narrow is the way, which leadeth unto life ; and few there be that find it.

Beware of false prophets, which come to you in sheep's clothing ; but inwardly they are ravening wolves. Ye shall know them by their fruits. Do men gather grapes of thorns, or figs of thistles ? Even so every good tree bringeth forth good fruit ; but a corrupt tree bringeth forth evil fruit. A good tree cannot bring forth evil fruit ; neither can a corrupt tree bring forth good fruit. Every tree that bringeth not forth good fruit is hewn down, and cast into the fire. Wherefore by their fruits ye shall know them.

SELECTION VII.

Hear the word of God as recorded in the fifty-third chapter of Isaiah.

WHO hath believed our report ? and to whom is the arm of the Lord revealed ? For he shall grow up before him as a tender plant, and as a root out of a dry ground ; he hath no form nor comeliness ; and when we shall see him, there is no beauty that we should desire him. He is despised and rejected of men, a man of sorrows, and acquainted with grief : and we hid as it were our faces from him ; he was despised, and we esteemed him not. Surely he hath borne our griefs, and carried our sorrows : yet we did esteem him stricken, smitten of God, and afflicted. But he was wounded for our transgressions, he was bruised for our iniquities : the chastisement of our peace was upon him ; and with his stripes we are healed. All we, like sheep, have gone astray ; we have turned every one to his own way ; and the Lord hath laid on him the iniquity of us all. He was oppressed, and he was afflicted; yet he opened not his mouth : he is brought as a lamb to the slaughter, and as a sheep before her shearers is dumb, so he openeth not his mouth. He was taken from prison and from judgment : and who shall declare his generation ? for he was cut off out of the land of the living : for the transgression of my people was he stricken. And he made his grave with the wicked, and with the rich in his death; because he had done no violence, neither was any deceit in his mouth. Yet it pleased the Lord to bruise him; he hath put him to grief : when thou shalt make his soul an offering for sin, he shall see his seed, he shall prolong his days, and the pleasure of the Lord shall prosper in his hand. He shall see of the travail of his soul, and shall be satisfied : by his knowledge shall my righteous servant justify many; for he shall bear their iniquities. Therefore will I divide him a portion with the great, and he shall divide the spoil with the strong; because he hath poured out his soul unto death; and he was numbered with the transgressors; and he bare the sin of many, and made intercession for the transgressors.

Hear again the word of God as recorded in the fifth chapter of Matthew.

AND seeing the multitudes, he went up into a mountain : and when he was set, his disciples came unto him : and he opened his mouth, and taught them, saying, Blessed are the poor in spirit : for theirs is the kingdom of heaven. Blessed are they that mourn : for they shall be comforted. Blessed are the meek : for they shall inherit the earth. Blessed are they which do hunger and thirst after righteousness : for they shall be filled. Blessed are the merciful : for they shall obtain mercy. Blessed are the pure in heart : for they shall see God. Blessed are the peace-makers : for they shall be called the children of God. Blessed are they which are persecuted for righteousness' sake : for theirs is the kingdom of heaven. Blessed are ye, when men shall revile you, and persecute you, and shall say all manner of evil against you falsely, for my sake. Rejoice, and be exceeding glad : for great is your reward in heaven : for so persecuted they the prophets which were before you.

Ye are the salt of the earth : but if the salt have lost his savour, wherewith shall it be salted ? It is thenceforth good for nothing, but to be cast out, and to be trodden under foot of men. Ye are the light of the world. A city that is set on a hill cannot be hid. Neither do men light a candle, and put it under a bushel, but on a candlestick ; and it giveth light unto all that are in the house. Let your light so shine before men, that they may see your good works, and glorify your Father which is in heaven.

SELECTION VIII.

Hear the word of God as recorded in the one hundred and third Psalm.

BLESS the Lord, O my soul ; and all that is within me, bless his holy name. Bless the Lord, O my soul, and forget not all his benefits : who forgiveth all thine iniquities; who healeth all thy diseases; who redeemeth thy life from destruction ; who crowneth thee with loving-kindness and tender mercies ; who satisfieth thy mouth with good things ; so that thy youth is renewed like the eagles. The Lord executeth righteousness and judgment for all that are oppressed. He made known his ways unto Moses, his acts unto the children of Israel. The Lord is merciful and gracious, slow to anger, and plenteous in mercy. He will not always chide; neither will he keep his anger for ever. He hath not dealt with us after our sins ; nor rewarded us according to our iniquities. For as the heaven is high above the earth, so great is his mercy towards them that fear him. As far as the east is from the west, so far hath he

4

removed our transgressions from us. Like as a father pitieth his children, so the Lord pitieth them that fear him. For he knoweth our frame; he remembereth that we are dust. As for man, his days are as grass : as a flower of the field, so he flourisheth. For the wind passeth over it, and it is gone; and the place thereof shall know it no more. But the mercy of the Lord is from everlasting to everlasting upon them that fear him, and his righteousness unto children's children; to such as keep his covenant, and to those that remember his commandments to do them. The Lord hath prepared his throne in the heavens; and his kingdom ruleth over all. Bless the Lord, ye his angels, that excel in strength, that do his commandments, hearkening unto the voice of his word. Bless ye the Lord, all ye his hosts; ye ministers of his, that do his pleasure. Bless the Lord, all his works in all places of his dominion : bless the Lord, O my soul.

Hear again the word of God as recorded in the third chapter of John.

AND as Moses lifted up the serpent in the wilderness, even so must the Son of man be lifted up; that whosoever believeth in him should not perish, but have eternal life.

For God so loved the world, that he gave his only begotten Son, that whosoever believeth in him should not perish, but have everlasting life. For God sent not his Son into the world to condemn the world : but that the world through him might be saved.

He that believeth on him, is not condemned : but he that believeth not, is condemned already, because he hath not believed in the name of the only begotten Son of God. And this is the condemnation, that light is come into the world, and men loved darkness rather than light, because their deeds were evil. For every one that doeth evil hateth the light, neither cometh to the light, lest his deeds should be reproved. But he that doeth truth, cometh to the light, that his deeds may be made manifest, that they are wrought in God.

SELECTION IX.

Hear the word of God as recorded in the fourth chapter of Proverbs.

ENTER not into the path of the wicked, and go not in the way of evil men. Avoid it, pass not by it, turn from it, and pass away. For they sleep not, except they have done mischief; and their sleep is taken away, unless they cause some to fall. For they eat the bread of wickedness, and drink the wine of violence. But the path of the just is as the shining light, that shineth more and more unto the perfect day. The way of the wicked is as darkness: they know not at what they stumble.

My son, attend to my words; incline thine ear unto my sayings. Let them not depart from thine eyes; keep them in the midst of thy heart. For they are life unto those that find them, and health to all their flesh.

Keep thy heart with all diligence; for out of it are the issues of life. Put away from thee a froward mouth, and perverse lips put far from thee. Let thine eyes look right on, and let thine eyelids look straight before thee. Ponder the path of thy feet, and let all thy ways be established. Turn not to the right hand nor to the left: remove thy foot from evil.

Hear again the word of God as recorded in the fourteenth chapter of John.

JESUS answered and said unto him, If a man love me, he will keep my words: and my Father will love him, and we will come unto him, and make our abode with him. He that loveth me not, keepeth not my sayings: and the word which ye hear is not mine, but the Father's which sent me. These things have I spoken unto you, being yet present with you. But the Comforter, which is the Holy Ghost, whom the Father will send in my name, he shall teach you all things, and bring all things to your remembrance, whatsoever I have said unto you. Peace I leave with you, my peace I give unto you : not as the world giveth, give I unto you. Let not your heart be troubled, neither let it be afraid. Ye have heard how I said unto you, I go away, and come again unto you. If ye loved me, ye would rejoice, because I said, I go unto the Father : for my Father is greater than I. And now I have told you before it come to pass, that when it is come to pass, ye might believe. Hereafter I will not talk much with you : for the prince of this world cometh, and hath nothing in me. But that the world may know that I love the Father; and as the Father gave me commandment, even so I do. Arise, let us go hence.

SELECTION X.

Hear the word of God as recorded in the seventh chapter of Ecclesiastes.

A GOOD name is better than precious ointment ; and the day of death than the day of one's birth. It is better to go to the house of mourning than to go to the house of feasting : for that is the end of all men; and the living will lay it to his heart. Sorrow is better than laughter : for by the sadness of the countenance the heart is made better. The heart of the wise is in the house of mourning : but the heart of fools is in the house of mirth. It is better to hear the rebuke of the wise, than for a man to hear the song of fools. For as the crackling of thorns under a pot, so is the laughter of the fool. This also is vanity. Surely oppression maketh a wise man mad ; and a gift destroyeth the heart. Better is the end of a thing than the beginning thereof; and the patient in spirit is better than the proud in spirit. Be not hasty in thy spirit to be angry : for anger resteth in the bosom of fools. Say not thou, What is the cause that the former days were better than these ? for thou dost not inquire wisely concerning this.

Wisdom is good with an inheritance; and by it there is profit to them that see the sun. For wisdom is a defence, and money is a defence : but the excellency of knowledge is that wisdom giveth life to them that have it. Consider the work of God : for who can make that straight which he hath made crooked? In the day of prosperity be joyful, but in the day of adversity consider : God also hath set the one over against the other, to the end that man should find nothing after him.

Hear again the word of God as recorded in the fourth chapter of the First Epistle of John.

BELOVED, let us love one another : for love is of God; and every one that loveth, is born of God, and knoweth God. He that loveth not knoweth not God; for God is love. In this was manifested the love of God toward us, because that God sent his only begotten Son into the world that we might live through him. Herein is love, not that we loved God, but that he loved us, and sent his Son to be the propitiation for our sins. Beloved, if God so loved us, we ought also to love one another. No man hath seen God at any time. If we love one another, God dwelleth in us, and his love is perfected in us. Hereby know we that we dwell in him, and he in us, because he hath given us of his Spirit. And we have seen, and do testify, that the Father sent the Son to be the Saviour of the world. Whosoever shall confess that Jesus is the Son of God, God dwelleth in him, and he in God.

SELECTION XI.

Hear the word of God as recorded in the ninety-sixth Psalm.

O SING unto the Lord a new song; sing unto the Lord all the earth. Sing unto the Lord, bless his name shew forth his salvation from day to day. Declare his glory among the heathen, his wonders among all people. For the Lord is great, and greatly to be praised : he is to be feared above all gods. For all the gods of the nations

4 *

are idols: but the Lord made the heavens. Honour and majesty are before him; strength and beauty are in his sanctuary. Give unto the Lord, O ye kindreds of the people, give unto the Lord glory and strength; give unto the Lord the glory due unto his name: bring an offering, and come into his courts. O worship the Lord in the beauty of holiness: fear before him all the earth. Say among the heathen, that the Lord reigneth: the world also shall be established that it shall not be moved: he shall judge the people righteously. Let the heavens rejoice, and let the earth be glad; let the sea roar, and the fulness thereof. Let the field be joyful, and all that is therein: then shall all the trees of the wood rejoice before the Lord: for he cometh, for he cometh to judge the earth: he shall judge the world with righteousness, and the people with his truth.

Hear again the word of God as recorded in the thirteenth chapter of the Epistle of Paul to the Romans.

RENDER therefore to all their dues; tribute to whom tribute is due; custom to whom custom; fear to whom fear; honour to whom honour. Owe no man any thing, but to love one another: for he that loveth another hath fulfilled the law. For this, Thou shalt not commit adultery, Thou shalt not kill, Thou shalt not steal, Thou shalt not bear false witness, Thou shalt not covet; and if there be any other commandment, it is briefly comprehended in this saying, namely, Thou shalt love thy neighbour as thyself. Love worketh no ill to his neighbour: therefore love is the fulfilling of the law. And that, knowing the time, that now it is high time to awake out of sleep: for now is our salvation nearer than when we believed. The night is far spent, the day is at hand: let us therefore cast off the works of darkness, and let us put on the armour of light. Let us walk honestly, as in the day; not in rioting and drunkenness, not in chambering and wantonness, not in strife and envying. But put ye on the Lord Jesus Christ, and make not provision for the flesh, to fulfil the lusts thereof.

SELECTION XII.

Hear the word of God as recorded in the seventeenth chapter
of Jeremiah.

THUS saith the Lord; Cursed be the man that trusteth
in man, and maketh flesh his arm, and whose heart
departeth from the Lord.   For he shall be like the heath
in the desert, and shall not see when good cometh; but
shall inhabit the parched places in the wilderness, in a
salt land and not inhabited.   Blessed is the man that
trusteth in the Lord, and whose hope the Lord is.   For
he shall be as a tree planted by the waters, and that
spreadeth out her roots by the river, and shall not see
when heat cometh, but her leaf shall be green; and shall
not be careful in the year of drought, neither shall cease
from yielding fruit.

The heart is deceitful above all things, and desperately
wicked: who can know it?   I the Lord search the heart,
I try the reins, even to give every man according to his
ways, and according to the fruit of his doings.   As the
partridge sitteth on eggs, and hatcheth them not; so he
that getteth riches, and not by right, shall leave them in
the midst of his days, and at his end shall be a fool.

A glorious high throne from the beginning is the place
of our sanctuary.   O Lord, the hope of Israel, all that
forsake thee shall be ashamed, and they that depart from
me shall be written in the earth, because they have forsaken the Lord, the fountain of living waters.   Heal me,
O Lord, and I shall be healed; save me, and I shall be
saved: for thou art my praise.

Hear again the word of God as recorded in the fifth chapter
of the First Epistle of Paul to the Thessalonians.

THEREFORE let us not sleep, as do others; but let
us watch and be sober.   For they that sleep, sleep
in the night; and they that be drunken, are drunken in
the night.   But let us, who are of the day, be sober, putting on the breast-plate of faith and love; and for a hel-

met, the hope of salvation.   For God hath not appointed us to wrath, but to obtain salvation by our Lord Jesus Christ, who died for us, that, whether we wake or sleep, we should live together with him.   Wherefore, comfort yourselves together, and edify one another, even as also ye do.   And we beseech you, brethren, to know them which labour among you, and are over you in the Lord, and admonish you; and to esteem them very highly in love for their work's sake.   And be at peace among yourselves.   Now we exhort you, brethren, warn them that are unruly, comfort the feeble-minded, support the weak, be patient toward all men.   See that none render evil for evil unto any man; but ever follow that which is good, both among yourselves, and to all men.   Rejoice evermore.   Pray without ceasing.   In every thing give thanks: for this is the will of God in Christ Jesus concerning you.   Quench not the Spirit.   Despise not prophesyings.   Prove all things; hold fast that which is good.   Abstain from all appearance of evil.   And the very God of peace sanctify you wholly; and I pray God your whole spirit and soul and body be preserved blameless unto the coming of our Lord Jesus Christ.

SELECTION XIII.

Hear the word of God as recorded in the nineteenth Psalm.

THE heavens declare the glory of God; and the firmament sheweth his handy-work.   Day unto day uttereth speech, night unto night sheweth knowledge.   There is no speech nor language, where their voice is not heard.   Their line is gone out through all the earth, and their words to the end of the world.   In them hath he set a tabernacle for the sun, which is as a bridegroom coming out of his chamber, and rejoiceth as a strong man to run a race.   His going forth is from the end of the heaven, and his circuit unto the ends of it: and there is nothing hid from the heat thereof.   The law of the Lord is perfect, converting the soul; the testimony of the Lord is sure, making wise the simple. The statutes of the Lord are right, rejoicing the heart: the commandment of the Lord is pure, enlightening the eyes. The fear of the Lord is clean, enduring for ever: the judgments of the Lord are true and righteous altogether. More to be desired are they than gold, yea, than much fine gold: sweeter also than honey and the honey-comb. Moreover, by them is thy servant warned: and in keeping of them there is great reward. Who can understand his errors? cleanse thou me from secret faults. Keep back thy servant also from presumptuous sins; let them not have dominion over me: then shall I be upright, and I shall be innocent from the great transgression. Let the words of my mouth, and the meditation of my heart, be acceptable in thy sight, O Lord, my strength, and my redeemer.

Hear again the word of God as recorded in the twenty-fifth chapter of Matthew.

WHEN the Son of man shall come in his glory, and all the holy angels with him, then shall he sit upon the throne of his glory: and before him shall be gathered all nations: and he shall separate them one from another, as a shepherd divideth his sheep from the goats: and he shall set the sheep on his right hand, but the goats on the left. Then shall the King say unto them on his right hand, Come, ye blessed of my Father, inherit the kingdom prepared for you from the foundation of the world: for I was a hungered, and ye gave me meat: I was thirsty, and ye gave me drink: I was a stranger, and ye took me in: naked, and ye clothed me: I was sick, and ye visited me: I was in prison, and ye came unto me. Then shall the righteous answer him, saying, Lord, when saw we thee a hungered, and fed thee? or thirsty, and gave thee drink? When saw we thee a stranger, and took thee in? or naked, and clothed thee? Or when saw we thee sick, or in prison, and came unto thee? And the King shall answer and say unto them, Verily I say unto you, Inasmuch as ye have done it unto one of the least of these my brethren, ye have done it unto me. Then shall he say also unto them on the left hand, Depart from me, ye cursed, into everlasting fire, prepared for the devil and his angels: for I was a hungered, and ye gave me no meat: I was thirsty, and ye gave me no drink: I was a stranger, and ye took me not in: naked, and ye clothed me not: sick, and in prison, and ye visited me not. Then shall they also answer him, saying, Lord, when saw we thee a hungered, or athirst, or a stranger, or naked, or sick, or in prison, and did not minister unto thee? Then shall he answer them, saying, Verily I say unto you, Inasmuch as ye did it not to one of the least of these, ye did it not to me. And these shall go away into everlasting punishment; but the righteous into life eternal.

SELECTION XIV.

Hear the word of God as recorded in the twenty-third chapter of Proverbs.

MY son, if thine heart be wise, my heart shall rejoice, even mine. Yea, my reins shall rejoice, when thy lips speak right things. Let not thine heart envy sinners, but be thou in the fear of the Lord all the day long. For surely there is an end; and thine expectation shall not be cut off. Hear thou, my son, and be wise, and guide thine heart in the way. Be not amongst wine-bibbers; amongst riotous eaters of flesh: for the drunkard and the glutton shall come to poverty; and drowsiness shall clothe a man with rags. Hearken unto thy father that begat thee, and despise not thy mother when she is old. Buy the truth, and sell it not; also wisdom, and instruction, and understanding. The father of the righteous shall greatly rejoice; and he that begetteth a wise child shall have joy of him. Thy father and thy mother shall be glad, and she that bare thee shall rejoice. My son, give me thine heart, and let thine eyes observe my ways. For an whore is a deep ditch; and a strange woman is a narrow pit. She also lieth in wait as for a prey, and increaseth the transgressors among men. Who hath woe? who hath sorrow? who hath contentions? who hath babbling? who hath wounds without cause? who hath redness of eyes? They that tarry long at the wine, they that go to seek mixed wine. Look not thou upon the wine when it is red, when it giveth his colour in the cup, when it moveth itself aright: at the last it biteth like a serpent, and stingeth like an adder. Thine eyes shall behold strange women, and thine heart shall utter perverse things : yea, thou shalt be as he that lieth down in the midst of the sea, or as he that lieth upon the top of the mast.

Hear again the word of God as recorded in the twelfth chapter of Luke.

FOR there is nothing covered, that shall not be re-vealed; neither hid, that shall not be known. Therefore, whatsoever ye have spoken in darkness shall be heard in the light; and that which ye have spoken in the ear in closets shall be proclaimed upon the house-tops. And I say unto you, my friends, Be not afraid of them that kill the body, and after that, have no more that they can do : but I will forewarn you whom ye shall fear : Fear him, which after he hath killed, hath power to cast into hell; yea, I say unto you, Fear him. Are not five sparrows sold for two farthings, and not one of them is forgotten before God? But even the very hairs of your head are all numbered. Fear not, therefore : ye are of more value than many sparrows. Also I say unto you, Whosoever shall confess me before men, him shall the Son of man also confess before the angels of God: but he that denieth me before men, shall be denied before the angels of God.

SELECTION XV.

Hear the word of God as recorded in the tenth chapter of
Deuteronomy.

AND now, Israel, what doth the Lord thy God require
of thee, but to fear the Lord thy God, to walk in
all his ways, and to love him, and to serve the Lord thy
God with all thy heart and with all thy soul, to keep the
commandments of the Lord, and his statutes, which I
command thee this day, for thy good ?   Behold, the heaven and the heaven of heavens is the Lord's thy God,
the earth also, with all that therein is.   Only the Lord
had a delight in thy fathers to love them, and he chose
their seed after them, even you above all people, as it is
this day.   Circumcise therefore the foreskin of your heart,
and be no more stiff-necked.   For the Lord your God is
God of gods and Lord of lords, a great God, a mighty,
and a terrible, which regardeth not persons, nor taketh
reward : he doth execute the judgment of the fatherless
and widow, and loveth the stranger, in giving him food
and raiment.   Love ye therefore the stranger : for ye
were strangers in the land of Egypt.   Thou shalt fear
the Lord thy God ; him shalt thou serve, and to him
shalt thou cleave, and swear by his name.   He is thy
praise, and he is thy God, that hath done for thee these
great and terrible things, which thine eyes have seen.

Hear again the word of God as recorded in the twelfth chapter
of the Epistle to the Romans.

LET love be without dissimulation.   Abhor that which
is evil ; cleave to that which is good.   Be kindly
affectioned one to another with brotherly love ; in honour
preferring one another ; not slothful in business ; fervent
in spirit ; serving the Lord ; rejoicing in hope ; patient
in tribulation ; continuing instant in prayer ; distributing
to the necessity of saints ; given to hospitality.   Bless
them which persecute you ; bless, and curse not.   Rejoice with them that do rejoice, and weep with them

that weep. Be of the same mind one toward another. Mind not high things, but condescend to men of low estate. Be not wise in your own conceits. Recompense to no man evil for evil. Provide things honest in the sight of all men. If it be possible, as much as lieth in you, live peaceably with all men. Dearly beloved, avenge not yourselves; but rather give place unto wrath: for it is written, Vengeance is mine; I will repay, saith the Lord. Therefore, if thine enemy hunger, feed him; if he thirst, give him drink: for in so doing thou shalt heap coals of fire on his head. Be not overcome of evil, but overcome evil with good.

SELECTION XVI.

Hear the word of God as recorded in the hundred and eleventh Psalm.

PRAISE ye the Lord. I will praise the Lord with my whole heart in the assembly of the upright, and in the congregation. The works of the Lord are great, sought out of all them that have pleasure therein. His work is honourable and glorious : and his righteousness endureth for ever. He hath made his wonderful works to be remembered : the Lord is gracious, and full of compassion. He hath given meat unto them that fear him : he will ever be mindful of his covenant. He hath showed the people the power of his works, that he may give them the heritage of the heathen. The works of his hands are verity and judgment : all his commandments are sure. They stand fast for ever and ever, and are done in truth and uprightness. He sent redemption unto his people ; he hath commanded his covenant for ever ; holy and reverend is his name. The fear of the Lord is the beginning of wisdom : a good understanding have all they that do his commandments : his praise endureth for ever.

5.

Hear again the word of God as recorded in the second chapter of
the Epistle to the Ephesians.

FOR by grace are ye saved through faith ; and that not
of yourselves ; it is the gift of God : not of works,
lest any man should boast.   For we are his workmanship,
created in Christ Jesus unto good works, which God hath
before ordained that we should walk in them.   Wherefore remember, that ye being in time past Gentiles in the
flesh, who are called Uncircumcision by that which is
called the Circumcision in the flesh made by hands ; that
at that time ye were without Christ, being aliens from
the commonwealth of Israel, and strangers from the cov-
enants of promise, having no hope, and without God in
the world : but now, in Christ Jesus, ye who sometimes
were far off, are made nigh by the blood of Christ.   For
he is our peace, who hath made both one, and hath
broken down the middle wall of partition between us ;
having abolished in his flesh the enmity, even the law
of commandments contained in ordinances ; for to make
in himself of twain one new man, so making peace ; and
that he might reconcile both unto God in one body by
the cross, having slain the enmity thereby ; and came and
preached peace to you which were afar off, and to them
that were nigh.   For through him we both have access by one Spirit unto the Father.   Now therefore ye
are no more strangers and foreigners, but fellow-citizens
with the saints, and of the household of God ; and are
built upon the foundation of the apostles and prophets,
Jesus Christ himself being the chief corner-stone ; in
whom all the building, fitly framed together, groweth
unto a holy temple in the Lord : in whom ye also are
builded together for a habitation of God through the
Spirit.

SELECTION XVII.

Hear the word of God as recorded in the first chapter of
Proverbs.

THE fear of the Lord is the beginning of knowledge:
but fools despise wisdom and instruction. My son,
hear the instruction of thy father, and forsake not the
law of thy mother : for they shall be an ornament of grace
unto thy head, and chains about thy neck. My son, if
sinners entice thee, consent thou not. If they say, Come
with us, let us lay wait for blood, let us lurk privily for
the innocent without cause : let us swallow them up
alive, as the grave ; and whole as those that go down
into the pit : we shall find all precious substance, we
shall fill our houses with spoil : cast in thy lot among us ;
let us all have one purse. My son, walk not thou in the
way with them ; refrain thy foot from their path : for
their feet run to evil, and make haste to shed blood :
(surely in vain the net is spread in the sight of any bird :)
and they lay wait for their own blood ; they lurk privily
for their own lives. So are the ways of every one that
is greedy of gain ; which taketh away the life of the
owners thereof. Wisdom crieth without ; she uttereth
her voice in the streets : she crieth in the chief place of
concourse, in the openings of the gates : in the city she
uttereth her words, saying, How long, ye simple ones,
will ye love simplicity, and the scorners delight in their
scorning, and fools hate knowledge ? Turn you at my reproof ; behold, I will pour out my Spirit unto you, I will
make known my words unto you.

Hear again the word of God as recorded in the fourth chapter
of the Epistle of James.

SUBMIT yourselves therefore to God. Resist the
devil, and he will flee from you. Draw nigh to
God, and he will draw nigh to you. Cleanse your hands,
ye sinners, and purify your hearts, ye double-minded.
Be afflicted, and mourn, and weep : let your laughter be

turned to mourning, and your joy to heaviness. Humble yourselves in the sight of the Lord, and he shall lift you up. Speak not evil one of another, brethren. He that speaketh evil of his brother, and judgeth his brother, speaketh evil of the law, and judgeth the law: but if thou judge the law, thou art not a doer of the law, but a judge. There is one Lawgiver, who is able to save, and to destroy: who art thou that judgest another? Go to now, ye that say, To-day or to-morrow we will go into such a city, and continue there a year, and buy, and sell, and get gain: whereas ye know not what shall be on the morrow. For what is your life? It is even a vapour, that appeareth for a little time, and then vanisheth away. For that ye ought to say, If the Lord will, we shall live, and do this, or that. But now ye rejoice in your boastings: all such rejoicing is evil. Therefore to him that knoweth to do good, and doeth it not, to him it is sin.

Selection XVIII.

Hear the word of God as recorded in the one hundred and sixteenth Psalm.

I LOVE the Lord, because he hath heard my voice and my supplications. Because he hath inclined his ear unto me, therefore will I call upon him as long as I live. The sorrows of death compassed me, and the pains of hell gat hold upon me: I found trouble and sorrow. Then called I upon the name of the Lord; O Lord, I beseech thee, deliver my soul. Gracious is the Lord, and righteous; yea, our God is merciful. The Lord preserveth the simple: I was brought low, and he helped me. Return unto thy rest, O my soul; for the Lord hath dealt bountifully with thee. For thou hast delivered my soul from death, mine eyes from tears, and my feet from falling. I will walk before the Lord in the land of the living. I believed, therefore have I spoken: I was greatly afflicted: I said in my haste, All men are liars. What shall I render unto the Lord for all his benefits toward me? I will take the cup of salvation, and call upon the name of the Lord. I will pay my vows unto the Lord now in the presence of all his people. Precious in the sight of the Lord is the death of his saints. O Lord, truly I am thy servant; I am thy servant, and the son of thy handmaid: thou hast loosed my bonds. I will offer to thee the sacrifice of thanksgiving, and will call upon the name of the Lord. I will pay my vows unto the Lord now in the presence of all his people, in the courts of the Lord's house, in the midst of thee, O Jerusalem. Praise ye the Lord.

Hear again the word of God as recorded in the first chapter of the First Epistle of Peter.

WHEREFORE gird up the loins of your mind, be sober, and hope to the end for the grace that is to be brought unto you at the revelation of Jesus Christ: as obedient children, not fashioning yourselves according to the former lusts in your ignorance. But as he which hath called you is holy, so be ye holy in all manner of conversation; because it is written, Be ye holy; for I am holy. And if ye call on the Father, who without respect of persons judgeth according to every man's work, pass the time of your sojourning here in fear: forasmuch as ye know that ye were not redeemed with corruptible things, as silver and gold, from your vain conversation received by tradition from your fathers; but with the precious blood of Christ, as of a lamb without blemish and without spot: who verily was fore-ordained before the foundation of the world, but was manifest in these last times for you, who by him do believe in God, that raised him up from the dead, and gave him glory; that your faith and hope might be in God. Seeing ye have purified your souls in obeying the truth through the Spirit unto unfeigned love of the brethren, see that ye love one another with a pure heart fervently: being born again, not of corruptible seed, but of incorruptible, by the word of God, which liveth and abideth for ever.

5 *

For all flesh is as grass, and all the glory of man as the flower of grass. The grass withereth, and the flower thereof falleth away but the word of the Lord endureth for ever. And this is the word which by the gospel is preached unto you.

PLAIN AND SHORT DISCOURSES

ON THE

PRINCIPAL DOCTRINES OF THE GOSPEL.

ABRIDGED FROM "VILLAGE SERMONS,"

BY GEORGE BURDER.

(55)

PLAIN AND SHORT DISCOURSES

ON THE

PRINCIPAL DOCTRINES OF THE GOSPEL.

SERMON I.

THE CONVERSION OF THE JAILER.

Acts xvi. 30, 31. Sirs, what must I do to be saved? And
they said, Believe on the Lord Jesus Christ, and thou shalt
be saved.

THE question I have read to you was asked by the
Jailer at Philippi, and the answer was given by Paul
and Silas.   The case was this : Paul and Silas were taken
up for preaching the gospel, and brought before the rulers.
The rulers unjustly caused them to be severely whipped,
and then " cast them into prison, charging the jailer to
keep them safely ; who, having received such a charge,
thrust them into the inner prison, and made their feet
fast in the stocks."

But these good men were not unhappy; their Master
was with them, according to his gracious promise, and
filled their hearts with joy ; so that, even at midnight,
they could not refrain from singing praises to God; and
their fellow-prisoners, in other dungeons, heard them with
surprise.

Just then, that God might show his regard to them,
and his anger against their persecutors, there was, all on

a sudden, a very great and awful earthquake, so that the foundations of the prison were shaken by it. At the same time, all the doors flew open; and all the bands and fetters that were on them, and the rest of the prisoners, dropped off at once.

The keeper of the jail, starting up from his sleep, and finding the prisoners at liberty, was so terrified lest he should be charged with a breach of trust in letting them escape, that he drew his sword, and was going to stab himself.

But Paul, knowing his wicked design, and moved with pity for him, though he had used them so ill, cried out aloud, " Do thyself no harm, for we are all here." The jailer, calling for a light, ran with all speed into the inner prison ; and being full of horror at such an appearance of God in favour of his servants, and, at the same time, struck by the Holy Spirit with a deep conviction of his own guilt and danger, he threw himself on the ground before them, and asked their direction for the relief of his soul, in the words of our text : " Sirs, what must I do to be saved ?" A more important question was never asked. It becomes every one to make the inquiry ; and if any one of you has never before seriously made it, God grant you may do so now! The answer given, and the only proper answer that could be given, was, " Believe on the Lord Jesus Christ, and thou shalt be saved." May the Lord assist us, while we consider these two parts of the text !

I. An important question.

II. A gospel answer.

I. The question. It is in few words, but they are full of meaning. Let us examine it. And I shall consider it, first,

As the language of conviction. By conviction, I mean the work of the Holy Spirit on the mind of a sinner, whereby he is convinced that he is a sinner, and is properly affected with it. Without this, people try to excuse or lessen their sins. Some lay the blame of their sin upon others, as Adam did upon Eve, and as Eve did upon the serpent. People in general think very little, and very lightly of their sin. Some even make a mock at sin, and glory in it. This is a sad state to be in. Such persons are very far from God, and have no religion at all, whatever they may pretend to have. Such were the Pharisees, who were thought to be very religious; but they generally despised and opposed Jesus Christ; for, as he told them, "the whole need not a physician, but those who are sick."

But it is a good thing to be sensible of our sin. It is the first work of God upon the soul to make us so. For this purpose we must consider the holy law of God contained in the Ten Commandments. "By the law is the knowledge of sin," and, "Sin is the transgression of the law." Thus Paul himself came to see he was a sinner, as he tells us, Rom. vii. 9. "I was alive without the law once; but when the commandment came, sin revived, and I died." If ever we have broken the law, even once in our lives, we are sinners; for as it is written, Gal. iii. 10. "Cursed is every one that continueth not in all things, written in the book of the law, to do them." Now *who* is there, that can pretend to say, he never sinned in all his life? Do you not confess, when you pray, that you are miserable sinners? But it is one thing to say so, merely in a customary way; and another, to be seriously convinced of it, and deeply affected with it.

The Holy Spirit not only brings us to admit, what we can hardly deny, that we have sinned; but he also shows us, that we have sinned much and often; that we have sinned in our hearts thousands of times, when we have not seemed to others to sin.

He also shows us the very great *evil* there is in sin. He shows us what abominable *ingratitude* there is in it; for "God has nourished us, and brought us up as chil-

dren, and we have rebelled against him." He shows
what a *base* and *filthy* thing sin is; that it makes us
hateful and abominable in his sight, viler than the brutes
that perish. And he also shows us the *danger* there is
in sin. "The wages of sin is death." Sin brought all
our miseries into the world. It is owing to sin that we
must all die, and return to dust; and, what is worse, sin
exposes us to the wrath of God and the flames of hell
for ever. Now the jailer saw all this, and therefore
cried out, "What must I do to be saved?" And this
leads me next to observe, that

This question bespeaks Fear. Yes, my brethren, it is
the language of fear: it is the language of terror and
consternation. Whenever we are alarmed at the approach
of some dreadful evil, it is natural to cry, What shall I
do? And have not sinners much to fear? Is it not "a
fearful thing to fall into the hands of the living God?"
Oh! consider who he is that we have provoked by our
sins. It is the great, the Almighty God, who made the
world with a word, and can crush it in a moment. It
is "the Lord, who hath his way in the whirlwind and
in the storm, and the clouds are the dust of his feet.
The mountains quake at him, and the hills melt, and the
earth is burned, at his presence. Who can stand before
his indignation? and who can abide the fierceness of his
anger?" Nahum i. 3—6. This is that dreadful God,
who hath said, "that the wicked shall be turned into
hell, with all who forget him." Shall we not fear him
then? Shall we not tremble at his presence? "Yea,"
saith the Lord, "I say unto you, Fear him who can not
only kill the body, but cast both body and soul into hell"
Oh! how would you shudder to see a fellow-creature burning at a stake! how would you wish that death would
speedily end his pain! But how would you feel, to see
him burn a whole hour, a whole day, a whole week, and
all the time filling the air with horrid shrieks, and crying in vain for ease or death? Horrid as this would be,

it gives but a faint idea of hell; that dreadful place of torment, " where the worm dieth not, and where the fire is not quenched." It was the dread of this that made the jailer cry, " What must I do to be saved?" And it was well for him, that he foresaw the evil, and found a refuge from it. God grant we may all do the same. But there is more in the question.

It is also the language of Desire; earnest, ardent, desire. The natural man desires only carnal things. What shall I eat, what shall I drink, what shall I wear? How may I be rich, and happy, and respected? or, as the psalmist expresses it, " Who will show me any good;" any worldly good, any temporary good? But " that which is born of the Spirit, is spirit." The awakened soul has new desires; or, rather, all his desires are brought into one, and that one is salvation. " What shall I do to be *saved?* to be delivered from the wrath to come; to have my sins pardoned; to be restored to the divine favor?" This is now " the one thing needful." Without this, all other things are of no value; they are less than nothing, and vanity, compared with salvation. This earnest desire will soon be expressed in prayer. For the sinner knows that salvation can come only from God; and, as it was remarked by Christ himself, concerning Saul when converted, " Behold, he prayeth!" so it will always be found, that the desire of the new-born soul will vent itself in prayer. Those who live without prayer, are strangers to this desire, and are totally destitute of religion.

Once more, we may observe, that the jailer's question includes a Confession of his Ignorance. He wanted to be saved, but he knew not *how;* nor can any man know this aright till he is taught of God. It is the true character of natural men, as mentioned, Rom. iii. 17, that " the way of peace they have not known." By the fall of man, in Adam, " darkness has covered the earth, and gross darkness the people." And this is the state,

6

not only of the blind Heathen, who have not the Bible, but of a great many called Christians. How many are there among *us*, who are entirely ignorant of the way in which poor sinners are saved by Jesus Christ! But, to remove this fatal darkness, Christ, the Sun of Righteousness, hath arisen upon the earth. He is the light of the world; and he has commanded his ministers to "preach the gospel to every creature." Paul and Silas were so employed before they were cast into prison. It had been declared in the city concerning them—"These men are the servants of the most High God, which show unto us the way of salvation," ver. 17. As soon, therefore, as the jailer was convinced of his need of salvation and his ignorance, he earnestly desires to be taught by them. He no longer reviles and abuses these ministers of Christ, but applies to them for instruction. And thus it will be with all who are truly serious. They will not mock at preachers of the gospel, but rather "stand in the way, and see, and ask for the old paths; where is the good way, that they may walk therein, and find rest for their souls," Jer. vi. 16. And now say, my friends, whether you have ever felt in your minds this earnest desire to know the way of God more perfectly. For this end, do you bow your knees to God in prayer? Do you read your Bible for this purpose? And with this view do you go to hear the ministers of Christ? Be assured, this is the pursuit of all who are under divine influence.

Finally, I consider this question as the language of Submission. Poor man! his heart was alarmed with fear, and humbled for sin. He saw nothing but eternal destruction before him, and would give all the world to avoid it: and therefore he cries, What shall I do? As if he had said, Show me my duty, and let it be ever so hard and difficult, I am ready to do it. I would go through fire or water, so that my precious soul may be saved. And is it so with *you?* Are you willing to part with your sins? Depend upon it you are not in the way to salvation till you are willing to part with all for Christ: and if you are, how gladly will you hear the true way to salvation, as declared by these inspired servants of our Lord! This is contained in the second part of our subject; or,

II. The gospel answer, given to the jailer's question. This short and plain answer is the only true one that can be given to the important inquiry; and it is of vast importance that a convinced soul be led in the right way.

Observe, *Who it is* that Paul recommends to the notice of this distressed man. It is the LORD JESUS CHRIST. It is the LORD—the maker of heaven and earth, Col. i. 16 ;—"the Lord of all," Acts x. 30, who came down from heaven. The "Son of God," who became "the Son of Man," that we, the children of men, might become the children of God. His name is called JESUS, which signifies a *Saviour*, and he was so called, because "he came to save us from our sins," Matt. i. 21. Yes, "this is, indeed, a faithful saying, and worthy of all acceptation, that Jesus came into the world to save sinners." He is also called CHRIST, or the Messiah, long promised, and long expected by the Jews; and it signifies the *Anointed*, which implies that he was every way qualified for the work of salvation, and appointed to it. This then is the glorious person, to whom a sinner is directed to look for salvation. Believe on the Lord Jesus Christ. . He exhorts him to *believe*. What is to believe on him? I answer, it is to believe all that God says in the gospel concerning him, so as to look to him alone for salvation. Faith is explained by *coming to Christ;* it is the application of the mind to him for relief. It is called *receiving Christ;* the soul accepts him as held forth in the gospel, in all his saving characters and offices. It is a *committing the soul* to him, knowing there is salvation in him, and in no other, and humbly relying on his love and faithfulness to preserve it unto eternal salvation. But the nature of faith will be more fully considered hereafter.

Observe, further, the comfortable assurance that is here given to the distressed jailer. *Thou shalt be saved.* Salvation was what he longed for. He wanted to know the way of it. He is directed to Jesus as the Saviour, and to believe on him, as the way of being saved by him; and in so doing, he is assured that salvation shall be his. Blessed be God for many precious promises to this purpose in his word. Hear what Jesus Christ himself saith, John iii. 36, "He that believeth on the Son hath everlasting life." And in another place, John vi. 40, "This is the will of him that sent me, that every one that seeth the Son, and believeth on him, may have everlasting life."

APPLICATION.—And now, my friends, let me ask you, Are you concerned about your souls? Were you ever brought, like the jailer, to ask, with seriousness, with earnestness of soul, What must I do to be saved? Are you not sinners? Are you not dying sinners? Must you not soon appear before your Judge? What, then, will you plead? Are you ready for the solemn trial? Oh, consider these things! trifle no longer with your souls! Eternity is at hand, heaven or hell will soon be your portion. And can you be unconcerned? Be assured, that serious consideration and deep conviction are absolutely necessary. There is no real religion without these. If you never felt a concern for the salvation of your souls—if you never felt a desire to know how you must be saved, you are yet strangers to any true religion. You are Christians only in name. You are far from God, and in a most dangerous condition. Oh then, look up to God for the teaching of his Spirit; beg him to take away your heart of stone, and to make you truly desirous of his salvation.

If you are concerned about your soul, which way do you look for help? If you would be saved, what course do you take? Do you say, "I must repent and reform?" It is true; so you must. But do you think that repentance, or reformation is sufficient to save your soul? No: Jesus is the only Saviour. The apostles directed sinners to believe in him. That is your first business. Pray for faith. It is the gift of God; and he will give it you, if you will ask him. And if you truly believe, repentance and reformation will surely follow, together with all good works, by which a true faith is as certainly known as a tree is discerned by its fruits. How soon did the jailer prove the truth of his faith in this manner! He showed the utmost readiness to hear the gospel preached by the ministers of Christ; and he joined to works of piety, those of charity; "he took Paul and Silas, the same hour of the night, and washed their stripes;" he also took upon himself the full profession of this new and despised religion, by being baptized, and so separating himself from all his heathen neighbours. Then let us immediately separate ourselves from the vain world, and boldly confess to whom we belong; while we show the strongest affection to the ministers and people of God.

SERMON II.

REGENERATION, OR THE NEW BIRTH.

John iii. 3. Jesus answered, and said unto him, Verily, verily, I say unto thee, Except a man be born again, he cannot see the kingdom of God.

THE *new birth* signifies a *great change*, made in the heart of a sinner by the power of the Holy Spirit. It means that something is done in us, and for us, which we cannot do for ourselves; something, to which we were before strangers; something, whereby we begin to live, as we did not live before; yea, something, whereby such a life begins as shall last for ever; for, as by our first birth we are born to die, so, by our second birth, we are born to live for ever.

That we may better understand the new birth, or this change of heart, let us more particularly consider,

I. The *nature* of this change; and,

II. The *necessity* of it.

I. Let us consider the *nature* of this change. "It is not a change of the substance and faculties of the soul. Sin did not destroy the essence of the soul, but its rectitude: so grace does not give a new faculty, but a new quality. It is not destroying the metal, but the old stamp upon it, to imprint a new one. It is not breaking the candlestick, but putting a new light in it. It is a new stringing the instrument, to make a new harmony.

It is a *great* change: or else such a term as "the new birth," or, "a new creation," or, "resurrection," would not be proper. The greatness of this change is elsewhere described by "passing from darkness to light;" yea, by "passing from death to life." "You hath he quickened, who were dead in trespasses and sins." It makes a man quite the contrary to what he was before, as contrary as East to West; North to South; light to darkness; flesh to spirit. It is such a change, as if a black man should become white; or a lion become a lamb. In a word, God takes away the heart of stone, and gives a heart of flesh.

It is an *inward* change. It will indeed produce an outward change, if the life was before immoral; but there may be strict morality without this inward change. Reformation is not Regeneration, though too often mistaken for it. It is a change of *heart*. We must be "renewed in the spirit of our mind," Eph. iv. 23. "Man looks at the outward appearance, but God looketh at the heart," God has promised to give his people "a new heart;" and the penitent psalmist prays for it—"Create in me a clean heart, O God! and renew a right spirit

within me." Without this there is no true change.
"The spring and wheels of a clock must be mended, before the hand of the dial will stand right. It may stand
right twice in the day, when the time of the day comes to
it, but not from any motion or rectitude in itself. So a
man may seem by one or two actions to be a changed
man; but the inward spring being amiss, it is but a deceit."
Many people abstain from some sins, and perform some
duties, for the sake of health, reputation, or profit; but
in the new creature there is a change of *principle*. The
principle of a new creature is faith, "faith working by
love," and this abides. He is not like a clock that is
wound up, and goes only while it is acted upon by the
weights; but, having the Spirit of God within him, and
the life of God in his soul, grace is as " a well of water,
springing up into everlasting life."

There is in the new creature a change of the *end* he
has in view, as well as the *principle* from which he acts.
"The glory of God is the end of the new man : *self* is
the end of the old man." Nothing is a greater evidence
of being born again, than to be taken off the old centre
of self, and to aim at the glory of God in everything,
whether we eat or drink, whether we are in private or
public, whether we are engaged in religious or in common
affairs ; to desire and aim sincerely at the glory of God ;
knowing that " we are not our own, but bought with a
price, we are to glorify God with our body, soul, and
spirit, all which are his."

He has new thoughts of *God*. Before, he lived, in a
great measure, " without God in the world ;" without any
true knowledge of God; without any proper regard to
God; and was ready to think God " altogether such a
one as himself." But now he sees that with God there
is " terrible majesty," perfect purity, strict justice, and
that he is indeed greatly to be feared. Now he knows
that God's eye is always upon him; and that, if He were
to enter into judgment with him, he could never stand.

But he learns also from the gospel, that God in Christ is full of grace, and goodness, and love; so that, " he fears the Lord and his goodness."

The new creature has very different thoughts of *himself*. He once acted as his own master; followed his own wicked will; was ready to excuse his worst actions; thought lightly of his sins; perhaps gloried in his shame. Now he sees the evil of his former ways; he mourns sincerely for his sins; he sees the badness of his heart from whence they flowed; he ranks himself among the chief of sinners; he wonders at his former boldness in sin; and he wonders more at the patience of God, in not cutting him off with some sudden stroke of his judgment. In short, he cries, " Behold, I am vile. I abhor myself, and repent in dust and ashes."

The new creature has new thoughts of the *world;* of the *men* of it, and the *things* of it. Once he loved the company of profane and unclean persons; now he shuns them as he would the plague; and his language is, " Depart from me, ye wicked men, for I will keep the commandments of my God." Before, he hated the very sight of a godly person; now, his heart unites with those who fear the Lord; he thinks them " the excellent of the earth," wishing to live and die with them. How different also are his views of the things of the world! Once they were his only portion. He sighed to be great; he longed to be rich; he panted for pleasure. Eating and drinking, cards and plays, music and dancing, or some other vain amusements, were his dear delight; and to enjoy these he would sacrifice everything. Now he sees the vanity of them all. He sees their danger. They had led him to the brink of ruin; and now he can truly say,

> " These pleasures now no longer please,
>   No more delight afford :
> Far from my heart be joys like these,
>   Now I have known the Lord !"

But oh, what new apprehensions has he of *Eternity !* He hardly ever used to think of it; now it is almost always on his mind; for now he has that *faith*, which is " the substance of things hoped for, the evidence of things not seen." Now, therefore, he looks not at the things that are seen, for he knows they are temporal; but at the things which are not seen, for they are eternal. He knows that he must live for ever; either in a glorious heaven, or in a dreadful hell. Compared, therefore, with eternal concerns, all worldly things appear as empty shadows, and he considers everything below according to the relation it bears to his eternal happiness.

The new creature has also very different thoughts of *Jesus Christ* from what he had before. Once he was without form and comeliness to him; now he appears " the chief among ten thousand, and altogether lovely." He did not wish to hear of him, or read of him, or speak of him, except to profane his name : now he can never hear enough of him ; for he sees, that if ever he is saved, he owes it all to Jesus, and therefore " counts all things but loss, that he may know him, and win him, and be found in him."

He also thinks very differently of *religious ordinances.* He could not bear to keep the Sabbath holy. Either he wholly neglected public worship, and took his carnal pleasure ; or if he came, it was a burden : he did not join in prayer ; singing, at best, was an amusement; he disregarded the word preached, perhaps derided it; and, as for private prayer, he hated it. How great the change ! Now the Sabbath is his delight, " the holy of the Lord and honourable." The house of God is his home; the word of God his food; the Bible his dear companion ; and prayer the breath of his soul.

Thus you see what a change has taken place in his *views ;* and, if time permitted, we might show that these *new views* are attended with *new affections ;* he loves what before he hated ; he hates what before he loved.

He has new desires, new fears, new joys, and new sorrows. He makes new resolutions. He is employed in new labours. He has new entertainments. He has new hopes and prospects. How justly then is he called a new creature!

Having briefly shown the *nature* of regeneration, let us consider,

II. The *necessity* of it. Observe how very strongly our Lord asserts in the text—"Verily, verily, I say unto thee, Except a man be born again, he cannot see the kingdom of God." Surely, these words must have great weight with us, if we believe the God of truth. But you will ask, What is meant by the kingdom of God? I answer, it means the kingdom of grace upon earth, and the kingdom of glory in heaven. Now, without the new birth, no person whatever can see the kingdom of God. It is not said, *he may not*, or *he shall not*, but he *cannot*; it is impossible in the nature of things.

He cannot perform any of the *duties*. Fallen man is ignorant of what is truly good. "He calls evil good, and good evil." He is, "to every good work, reprobate," Titus i. 16. And he has a dislike to that which is good. "The carnal mind is enmity against God," and shows its enmity by rebellion against the law of God, Rom. viii. 7. Now, remaining in this state, he cannot answer the end of his being, which is to glorify God; and having this unfitness and unwillingness to answer that end, there is an absolute, a universal necessity for this change. It is "in Christ Jesus we are created to good works." We cannot "pray in the Spirit," till we are "born of the Spirit;" we cannot "sing with grace in our hearts," till we have grace; we cannot worship God in the Spirit," while we are in the flesh. A dead sinner cannot present "a living sacrifice." The duties of a natural man are lifeless and selfish; "he cannot serve God spiritually," because he is carnal; nor graciously, for he is corrupt; nor vitally, because he is dead; nor freely, for he is enmity against God; nor delightfully, for his heart is alienated; nor sincerely, for his heart is deceit; nor acceptably, " for he that is in the flesh cannot please God."

In like manner the unregenerate person cannot enjoy any of the blessed *privileges* of the gospel state. He knows nothing of the joys of salvation. He is a stranger to the peace of the gospel. He has no relish for the sincere milk of the word. He cannot delight in prayer; nor enjoy communion with God, or communion with the saints, for things that are not natural can never be delightful. And this also makes it plain, that

The unrenewed man cannot see the kingdom of *glory*. The new birth does not indeed entitle a person to heaven; but it makes him " meet for the inheritance of the saints in light." The unrenewed sinner is shut out from heaven by the unalterable determination of God himself, who has declared, that " nothing which defileth" shall enter that place, and that " without holiness no man shall see the Lord."

And if you consider what the joys and employments of heaven are, and what the disposition of a sinner is, it will plainly appear that he cannot see the kingdom of God. " The happiness of heaven is holiness; and to talk of being happy without it, is as great nonsense as to talk of being well without health, or being saved without salvation." People are ready to think, if they go to heaven they must be happy; but, without a new nature, a man might be as much out of his element in heaven, as a fish, out of the bottom of the sea, would be in a green meadow, or an ox in the bottom of the sea. Can a wicked man, who now hates the godly, expect to be happy among none but saints? Can he, who cannot keep three hours of the Sabbath holy, bear to keep an eternal Sabbath? Can he, who now curses and swears, imagine that his tongue shall be for ever employed in praising God? Can he, who now hates to think of God, love to employ his mind in the eternal contemplation of him? No, no. Hell is the sinner's "own place;" there he will have his own company, and, in some measure, his old employments, though without the pleasure of them; but as to heaven, he can never see it till he be born again.

APPLICATION.—From what was first said of the nature of the new birth, let us learn to avoid the common mistake, that baptism is regeneration. It is the sign of it, but not the thing itself. We must " be born of water and of the Spirit," John iii. 5; that is, of the Holy Spirit, whose grace is to the soul, what water is to the body. Take not the shadow for the substance. Can baptism change the heart? Has it changed *yours?* Say, poor sinner, how is it with you? Conscience will tell you, "Old things are not passed away; all things are not become new." Do any of you live in drunkenness, profaneness, Sabbath-breaking, whoredom, or any other sin? Or do you live unconcerned about your soul, careless about salvation, without Christ, without prayer? Know for certain, that you are yet a stranger to this great and blessed change. And yet without it, the God of truth assures you, it is impossible for you to be saved. You must be born again. Do not think that outward reformation, or morality, or religious professions, or religious duties, are sufficient. All these are far short of this inward, spiritual change. You must be born again. As sure as there is a God in heaven, you must be born again, or you can never go to heaven. And can you bear the thought of being shut out? Put the question to yourself. "Can I dwell with everlasting burnings? Can I endure eternal darkness? Can I bear to be eternally separated from the blessed God? Is my present sinful, sensual life to be preferred before eternal joys? Is there one text in the Bible to give me comfort in this state?" Oh, that you may be so deeply convinced of the immediate necessity of this change, that you may, ere you sleep this night, fall down on your knees before God, and earnestly desire him to make you a new creature! He can do it in a moment; and he has promised his Holy Spirit to them that ask him.

SERMON III.

REPENTANCE

Mark vi. 12. And they went out, and preached that men should repent.

IT is remarkable, that whatever different notions men have of religion, they all believe that repentance is necessary to salvation. But it may be feared, that many mistake its true nature, and take the shadow for the substance. There are also many, who, though they think it necessary, delay their repentance to some future period; and more than a few die without it, and perish in their sins. It is therefore of great importance, that we should know wherein *true repentance* consists; and that we should be urged ourselves to repent, that we perish not. *That* repentance, then, which is true and genuine, and " needeth not to be repented of" will be found to include the four following things :

I. Conviction of sin.

II. Contrition for sin.

III. Confession of sin.

IV. Conversion from sin.

I. The first thing that belongs to true repentance is a conviction of sin, or a clear sight and feeling sense of our sinfulness; without this, there is no repentance, no religion; for the gospel may be justly called " the religion of a sinner;" none but sinners can need mercy or repentance; and Jesus Christ expressly declares, " that he came not to call the righteous," that is, such as the Pharisees, who *thought* themselves righteous, " but sinners to repentance." Now all men are sinners; not the most profane and openly wicked only, but the most moral, religious, and blameless people among us : for " all have sinned, and come short of the glory of God."

In general, the repenting sinner is first alarmed on account of some great and open sin, if he has committed such; as the woman of Samaria, when Christ charged her with adultery; or as Paul was, when convinced of his murderous persecution of the saints. But conviction will not stop here; it will trace the streams of sin to the spring, namely, that corrupt nature we brought into the world with us. We shall freely confess with David, that "we were born in sin, and in iniquity did our mothers conceive us," Psalm li. 5. We shall acknowledge with Paul, that "in us, that is, in our flesh," our corrupt nature, "there is no good thing;" but that "every imagination of the thought of our hearts is only evil continually," Gen. vi. 5. The penitent will readily own he has been a rebel against God all his life; that he has indeed "left undone those things which he ought to have done, and done those things which he ought not to have done."

The law of God is spiritual; it reaches to the most secret thoughts, desires, wishes, and purposes of the mind. It forbids and condemns the sins of the heart, as well as those of the lip and the life. A convinced sinner is sensible of heart-sins, thousands and millions of them. He sees that his best duties and services are mingled with sin; even his prayers, and all his religious exercises. He sees that he has, all his life, lived without God in the world, and paid no regard to his will and glory; that he has loved himself, the world, and the creature, far more than God; and that he has been doing all this contrary to light and knowledge; notwithstanding the checks of his conscience, and many resolutions to the contrary, and notwithstanding the mercies and the judgments which God had sent to reclaim him. Wherever there is this conviction, it will be accompanied with contrition.

II. Contrition, or *a genuine sorrow for sin*, and pain of heart on account of it. This is that "soft heart," or "heart of flesh," which God has promised to give his people; instead of that heart of stone, with which we are born, and which has no spiritual feeling.

"The sacrifices of God are a broken spirit: a broken and a contrite heart, O God, thou wilt not despise," Psalm li. 17. Men despise broken things. So the Pharisee despised the broken-hearted Publican in the temple; but God did not despise him. So far from it, that he accounts the sorrow and shame of a penitent sinner more valuable than many costly sacrifices of rams and bullocks. A heart that trembles at the word of God; a heart breaking, not in despair, but in humiliation; a heart breaking with itself, and breaking away from sin. So Peter, when duly affected with the sin of denying his master, "went out and wept bitterly;" and Mary Magdalene, sensible of former iniquities, washed her Saviour's feet with her tears.

There is indeed *a false sorrow*, which many mistake for the true. When a person is sick, and fears he shall die, it is not uncommon to hear him say he is sorry for sin; and if God will spare his life, he will amend his ways. But, too often, such a one is only sorry that God is so holy, that the law is so strict, and that he is in danger of being damned for his sins. He is not grieved that he has offended God, his best friend and benefactor, who has followed him with goodness and mercy all his life. But the rottenness of this repentance often appears when the sick person recovers; when the fright is over, he returns to the same carnal course as before. The sorrow is no better than that of some criminals at the gallows: very sorry they are that they have forfeited their lives; but they are not affected with the criminality of their actions. Felix trembled, but did not repent; and Judas was sorry for what he had done, but not in a godly manner. And this shows how very uncertain, for the most part, is the repentance of a dying bed. God forbid we should delay our repentance to that season!

But the sorrow of a true penitent is for *sin*, as committed against a holy and good God. Such was the penitence of David, who says, Psalm li. 4, "Against thee only have I sinned, and done this evil in thy sight." It is true that he had sinned against his fellow-creatures; against Uriah, and Bathsheba, and Joab, and all Israel: doubtless he lamented this; but what cut him to the heart, was his sin against God; *that* God who had raised him from the sheepfold to the throne; who had saved him from the hand of Saul, and given him his master's house; and if that had been too little, would have given him more; (for thus Nathan the prophet aggravated his sin.) "Against thee, O Lord," said the broken-hearted penitent, "against thee have I sinned." Thus, "the goodness of God led him to repentance." Observe, likewise, the tone of the returning prodigal. "I will arise, and go to my father, and say, Father, I have sinned against heaven, and in thy sight, and am no more worthy to be called thy son" He might have said, Sir, I have spent my fortune, hurt my health, become a beggar, and am ready to starve; be pleased to relieve me. No; his heart was affected with his sin and his folly. So it is with a repenting sinner. He considers the majesty of that holy being he has offended, the reasonableness of his command, the obligation he has broken through, and especially the base ingratitude of his conduct.

The goodness of God to a sinner, in the way of providence, may well excite this godly sorrow; but, how much more the consideration of redeeming love! What! did God "so love the world of rebel men as to send them his only begotten Son?" And did he send his Son, "not to condemn the world, but that the world through him might be saved?" O love beyond degree, beyond example, beyond expression!

Let the penitent also remember Jesus—the innocent, the amiable, the benevolent Jesus. Jesus, who left his throne of glory, and became a poor and afflicted man. Why was he despised and rejected of men? Why a man of sorrows and acquainted with grief? Why had he not a place where to lay his blessed head? Why did he endure the contradiction of sinners? Why was he oppressed and afflicted? Why was his visage so marred more than any man, and his form than the sons of men? I know the reason, may the weeping penitent say, " Surely he has borne my griefs, and carried my sorrows ; he was wounded for my transgressions, and bruised for my iniquities."

> " 'Twas you. my sins, my cruel sins,
> His chief tormenters were ;
> Each of my crimes became a nail,
> And unbelief the spear.

> " 'Twas you that pull'd the vengeance down,
> Upon his guiltless head ,
> Break, break, my heart, O burst, mine eyes,
> And let my sorrows bleed."

III. Confession of sin will also be made by the true penitent. By nature we are rather disposed to conceal, deny, and excuse our sins; to say we are no worse than others ; that we could not help committing them ; and that we see no great harm in them. But it is not so, where true repentance is found. We shall take the advice that Joshua gave to Achan " My son, give glory to the Lord, and make confession to him." To hide or deny our sins, is to dishonour God, as if he did not see, or would not punish it ; but to confess our sins, is to honour his holy law, which we have broken ; to honour his omniscience, which beheld all our crimes ; to honour his justice, which might take vengeance upon them ; and to honour his patience, which has forborne to strike the fatal blow. And indeed, a frank and free confession of our sins is the best way of finding peace. " When I kept silence," says the psalmist, " my bones waxed old through my roaring all the day long ; but I acknowledged my sin to thee, mine iniquity have I not hid ; I said, I will confess my transgressions to the Lord, and thou forgavest the iniquity of my sin " Psalm xxxii. 3, 5.

7 *

Secret sins require only secret confession to that God who seeth in secret; but sins that are public and scandalous ought to be more openly acknowledged, that we may undo, as far as we can, the evil committed.

The true penitent is *sincere* in his public confessions. How many call themselves "miserable sinners," declare that "the remembrance of their sins is grievous, and the burden of them intolerable;" and cry, "Lord have mercy upon us, Christ have mercy upon us," without the least sense of evil or burden of iniquity! This is abominable hypocrisy, and adding sin to sin. But the renewed soul is truly sincere in his confessions; he finds the words of Scripture well adapted to his feelings, and can cordially adopt those of Job, "Behold I am vile; I abhor myself, and repent in dust and ashes;" or the words of the Publican, "God be merciful to me, a sinner;" or the words of Paul, who calls himself "the chief of sinners."

We have now considered Conviction, Contrition, and Confession, as three essential ingredients in true repentance; and to these we must add one more:

IV. Conversion; which is a forsaking sin, and turning from it to God. John the Baptist, that great preacher of repentance, exhorted his hearers to "bring forth fruits meet for repentance." And thus Paul preached both to Jews and Gentiles, "that they should repent and turn to God, and do works meet for repentance," Acts xxvi. 20. Without this, the most humbling expressions and confessions, the greatest alarms of conscience or floods of tears, will prove insufficient. "Though Cain's terror, Judas's confession, Pharaoh's promises, Ahab's humiliation, Herod's hearing John gladly, and doing many things, were all combined in one man, they would not prove him a real penitent, while the love of one sin remained unmortified in the heart, or the practice of it *allowed* in his life." True repentance is not content to lop off the branches, but "lays the axe at the root of the

tree." The devil may suggest that a beloved sin is but
a little one, and may be spared; but grace will know,
that as one small leak may sink a ship, so one indulged
sin may damn a soul. However dear therefore a lust may
be, or however hard to be parted with, it must be
forsaken. So our Lord directs : " If thy right eye offend thee, pluck it out; if thy right hand offend thee,
cut it off;" that is, if thine eye or thine hand *cause thee to
offend*, or incline thee to sin, turn away thine eye from
it, as if thou hadst no eye to see it, or hand to practise
it; and be as willing to part with a beloved lust, as a
man who has a mortified hand or foot is willing to part
with it, to preserve his life " For it is better to enter
into life thus maimed, than having two eyes or two hands,
to be cast into hell, where the worm dieth not, and the
fire is not quenched."

You have a fine instance of true repentance in Zacche-
us, the converted Publican. When Christ and salvation
came to his house and heart, he, who had probably been
a great sinner, stands and says to the Lord, Behold,
Lord, the half of my goods I give to the poor; and if I
have taken anything from any man by false accusation, I
restore him four-fold." Here was not only confession of
sin, but forsaking it. He, who had been an extortioner,
becomes not only honest, but liberal. He makes *resti-
tution;* and so will every true penitent. He will undo
what he has done, if possible. Alas, how many evils is
it now impossible to undo! Some poor souls are perhaps in hell, to whose destruction our wickedness con-
tributed. But grace will enable us to do what is possible; sin shall not have dominion ; and we shall now be
as earnest to please and serve God, as once we were to
serve the devil

APPLICATION.—Come, then, and be encouraged to instant repentance. God might have cut you off in your sins,
without a moment's warning : but he has given you time
and space for repentance. His very command is encourage-

ment. It implies, that " there is forgiveness with him;"
pardon of sin and repentance are inseparably connected.
" Christ is exalted to give repentance and remission of
sins." " Let the wicked forsake his way, and the unrighteous man his thoughts ; and let him return unto the Lord,
and he will have mercy upon him, and to our God, for he
will abundantly pardon." Only do not suppose that repentance deserves or merits pardon. Salvation is all of
grace; but this is the order appointed of God ; for by
penitential sorrow, the heart is prepared to receive the
mercy of God through Jesus Christ our Lord.

Let the " goodness of God lead thee to repentance."
He delighteth not in the death of a sinner, but rather
rejoiceth in his return. And our Saviour assures us, that
" there is joy in heaven over one sinner that repenteth,
more than over ninety and nine just persons who need no
repentance " Arise, sinner, for he calleth thee. Does
your heart begin to relent? Are you saying, I will arise,
and go to my father? Arise, then, and go at once. He
will see thee afar off, and run to meet thee ; he waits to
be gracious, and there shall be joy in heaven, and joy on
earth, upon thy return.

Thousands as vile and base as you have found mercy.
Let not Satan say it is too late; the door is open : nor
let him say it is too soon. He may say, to-morrow will
do. God says, to-day; " while it is called to-day," then,
hear his voice. To-morrow may be too late. " This
night may thy soul be required of thee." Beware of de-
ferring repentance to a dying bed. Will you not then
have enough to do, to bear with patience the pain and
agonies of dissolving nature? Why should you plant
thorns in your dying pillow ? Why should you not then
have the peace of God, and the joy of the Holy Ghost,
to support and comfort your heart ? Who can tell but
sudden death may be your lot ? if not, extreme pain, or a
disordered head, may prevent the possibility of repentance. And do not imagine that repentance has anything

in it forbidding. Christ has said, "Blessed are they that mourn, for they shall be comforted." The penitent has more pleasure in his tears, than the worldling in all his gayety. Besides, if the door be strait, it opens into boundless pleasures; pleasures not confined to time, but which will last to all eternity. God now dwells in the contrite heart; and soon shall every true penitent dwell with him in paradise.

SERMON IV.

THE PHARISEE AND THE PUBLICAN.

Luke xvi. 16.—God be merciful to me a sinner.

OUR Saviour spake this parable unto certain which trusted in themselves that they were righteous, and despised others. Here are two bad things in their character. 1. *They trusted in themselves*—which no man can do, if he knows the holy law of God; and 2. *They despised others*, which we cannot do, if we know our own hearts. The conclusion shows how God dislikes such people, while he accepts a poor dejected sinner; for " every one that exalteth himself shall be abased; and he that humbleth himself shall be exalted." Ver. 14.

" Two men went up into the temple to pray : the one a Pharisee, and the other a Publican." Ver. 10. The Pharisees were a sect of people in those days in high repute for religion; they separated themselves from others, as if more holy : they distinguished themselves by peculiar zeal for ceremonies : but many of them were rank hypocrites, neglecting the religion of the heart, and indulging themselves in cruelty and oppression. The Publican also appeared at the same place, at the same time, and on the same errand; but how different their characters! Had we seen them both together, we should perhaps have thought far better of the Pharisee than of the Publican; "for man looketh only at the outward appearance, but God looketh at the heart." Very different motives brought them here. The Pharisee came because it was a public place, and he wished to be seen and admired ; the Publican came because it was "a house of prayer," and he wanted to pour forth his soul before God.

"And the Publican, standing afar off, would not lift up so much as his eyes to heaven, but smote upon his breast, saying, God be merciful to me a sinner !" By a *Publican* you are not to understand the keeper of a public-house, but a tax-gatherer. The Jews were at this time subject to the Roman emperor, and paid him taxes, which were sometimes farmed by the rich publicans, who, in the execution of their office, were too often dishonest and oppressive ; on account of which, and on account of the taxes themselves, which were vexatious to the Jews, the name of a publican was abominable, and was classed with those of harlots and sinners.

Whether this Publican was an extortioner, or not, we cannot say. Doubtless he was a sinner; and by some means or other he became a convinced sinner, a penitent sinner, and a praying sinner. Perhaps this was the first time that ever he prayed in his life ; for sinning generally keeps men from praying. It is plain that the Spirit of God had humbled his heart; and he was one of those blessed men, who are "poor in spirit," and he was one of those blessed mourners, who "shall be comforted."

Observe his posture—*he stood afar off*—at a great distance from the holy place, where the priest officiated ; he knew this became him, for he had lived at a great distance from God as a sinner ; and he knew he deserved that God should for ever behold him afar off.

Observe also his dejected looks : he could not look up ; he thought it would be presumptuous in him to lift up his eyes to heaven, the habitation of God's glory. Other sinners have thought the same ; David says, Ps. xl. 12,

"Innumerable evils have compassed me about; mine iniquities have taken hold upon me, so that I am not able to look up;" but those downcast eyes attracted the eyes of God; he could not lift up his eyes, but he lifted up his heart; and there is no beauty in the sight of God greater than blushing for sin. "For to this man will I look," saith the Lord, "even to him that is poor, and of a contrite spirit, and trembleth at my word." Isa. lxv. 2.

Another mark of his repentance was his *smiting his breast;* he knew his heart; he did not think it *a good heart*, as some very ignorant people speak; no, he knew the plague of his heart; he knew it was the seat and source of all his sins, and by smiting on his breast he seemed as if he would take revenge upon his own wicked heart; it expresses his indignation against himself, and the vehemence of his anger against sin. Men and brethren, what do you know of such a disposition as this? When were you thus angry with yourselves, and filled with shame and confusion of face because of your sins? Know this, that such is the temper of all who are taught of God; and if you have never felt in this manner, you are yet strangers to true repentance.

Now we come to his prayer. It was very short, but very good : no man ever offered a better, or to better purpose. Not that the mere words are of any avail: too many people use such words profanely, when they say, on a surprise, God bless us! or Lord have mercy on us! but such praying as this is the way to get a curse, not a blessing. When the Publican said, God be merciful to me, a sinner, he felt what he said : he felt he was a perishing sinner, and he felt an earnest desire for mercy.

He calls himself, *a sinner*, or *the sinner*, as some would render it; or *the chief of sinners*, as Paul called himself. The word *sinner* was a term of reproach among the Jews, and seemed to be applied chiefly to a harlot, or some notorious offender; but the Publican takes it to himself. It is very likely he spake this aloud in the hearing of the

Pharisee, and others who did not think themselves sinners; for he was not unwilling to appear before men what he well knew he was before God. He would not have been angry with that sort of preaching which lays men low; nor would he have been displeased with a friend who should have said, You are a very great sinner. But say, my friends, what would *you* think of a person who should charge *you* in that manner? Would you not be very angry, and say, I am no worse than others? But a true penitent can never find words sufficient to express the sense he has of his vileness.

If we know the meaning and extent of the Ten Commandments, we shall say after each of them, "Lord have mercy upon us!" And if we see anything of the holiness, majesty, and glory of the great God, we shall cry, with Isaiah, "Woe is me, for I am undone;" or with Job, "I have heard of thee by the hearing of the ear, but now mine eye seeth thee; wherefore I abhor myself, and repent in dust and ashes." No person truly enlightened will say, as many have done, I am not a great sinner; for, in fact, there cannot be a little sinner, unless there were a little law to break, a little God to offend, and a little wrath to incur. It is too common for persons to comfort themselves with the idea that they are not such great sinners as some others; many dying people do this, and even wretches at the gallows have done so. But this is very absurd; for the question is, not whether we have sinned as much as others, but whether we have sinned at all; that is, whether we have broken the holy law of God! If so, we are sinners, and stand exposed to the just wrath of the Most High; nor can we escape it but by partaking of that great mercy for which the Publican prayed.

You will next observe, that his sense of sin and danger put him upon prayer. Many people live without prayer; and what is the reason? They do not feel the need of mercy; for this is the first thing a convinced sinner prays for; and it is a good sign of grace, when a desire for mercy sends a man to his knees. Angels rejoice on such an occasion, and point to the new-born soul, saying, "Behold, he prayeth!" My friends, do you pray for mercy? If not, how can you expect it; and what must become of you without it? Oh that you may begin to pray!

This poor man cried to the Lord; and whither can a creature fly for help but to God? He is our maker; he is our governor; he is our just Judge; he is able to save or destroy: he is offended with our sins, yet is he most gracious, and ready to forgive. How reasonable, then, that a guilty, helpless sinner, ready to perish, should apply "to him that is able to save to the uttermost all who come to him by Jesus Christ!"

He begs for MERCY. What is mercy? We know what it is by our own feelings. It is compassion to the miserable; it is a disposition to pity and relieve the distressed; and we never speak of *mercy* but with reference to *misery*. It is not, then, a light, unfeeling use of solemn words, that can encourage us to hope for mercy: it is not saying, without feeling, Lord have mercy upon us! Christ have mercy upon us! but it is coming with the Publican's spirit, with his broken heart, with his remorse, with his desires, and in earnest prayer claiming this precious blessing.

Observe it is *mercy* he asks. Here is not a word of *merit*. Mercy and merit are opposite things. The Pharisee's prayer was a mere boast of meritorious deeds; the Publican has nothing to plead; nor does he ask for wealth, or honour, or pleasure; his heart is dead to these: all his desires centre in one, and that one is mercy.

> " Mercy, good Lord, mercy I ask,
> This is the total sum;
> For mercy, Lord, is all my suit
> Oh let thy mercy come!"

But the petition, *be merciful*, includes something more
8

than is commonly understood by it; the word translated
merciful has respect to the atonement made by blood; to
the sacrifice offered up at the temple; which were types
of Christ, " whom God hath set forth to be a propitiation, through faith in his blood." Rom. iii. 25. At the
temple, in the court of which the Publican stood, there
was a lamb offered every morning at nine o'clock, and
every evening at three; and these were the hours of
prayer; so that the pious Jews came then to pray, that
by virtue of the atonement of Christ represented by blood,
and of his intercession represented by the incense, their
prayers might find acceptance. His prayer then was—
God be propitious to me a sinner—accept the atonement
in my behalf—let my soul be cleansed in the blood of
Christ. In this manner, by faith in Jesus, let us seek
the mercy of God. Let us not dream of mere absolute
mercy. " A God all mercy is a God unjust " The
mercy of God cannot be bestowed without regard to his
justice. Now God has glorified his justice by punishing
sin in the person of our glorious Redeemer, upon whom
" he laid the iniquities of us all," and through whom he is,
at once, " a just God and a Saviour." In this way, and
in no other, can a sinner obtain mercy; for our Lord declares, that no man cometh to the Father but by him;
and no mercy cometh to the sinner but through him;
but in his dear name we may " come boldly to the throne
of grace, and so obtain mercy, and find grace to help in
every time of need."

Thus came the Publican, and in this way he succeeded.
It was not the depth of his humility, the sincerity of his
repentance, nor the fervency of his devotion, that merited
acceptance; these dispositions were the gifts of God, and
could merit nothing; but it was the merit of the Redeemer's precious blood, typified by the blood of lambs,
which he pleaded, and which shall never be pleaded in
vain. Our Lord tells us, ver. 14, " This man went down
to his house justified *rather* than the other," or *not the*

other; the reason of which he adds, " For every one that exalteth himself shall be abased ; and he that humbleth himself shall be exalted." Oh, what a blessing ! " He went down to his house justified ;" there was no condemnation to him ; he was accepted in the Beloved ; he had passed from death to life ! Happy man ! he might " eat his bread with gladness, and drink his wine," or water either, " with a merry heart, for God accepted his works."

APPLICATION.—Shall we not then " go and do likewise ?" Are we not sinners? Fly instantly to the throne of grace. The Lord waits to be gracious. This is the accepted time ; lose it not by delay. To-morrow may be too late. Now, then, with the Publican's spirit, let each of us cry, God be merciful to me a sinner !

But Oh ! beware of the Pharisee's spirit. Every man is born a Pharisee. Ask your little children why they hope to go to heaven; and if they have not been better taught, you will find their hope is, because they are not so bad as others. Would to God it were not so with grown-up persons too ! But let no one dare to persist in a self-righteous course ; " for he that exalteth himself shall be abased"—abased even to hell. Renounce, then, your own righteousness, as Paul, the converted Pharisee, did, who says, Phil. iii. 7, " What things were *gain* to me, those I counted loss for Christ; yea, doubtless, and I count all things but loss for the excellency of the knowledge of Christ Jesus my Lord, for whom I have suffered the loss of all things, and do count them but *dung,* that I may win Christ, and be found in him."

The Publican's success is a great encouragement to every sensible sinner seeking for mercy. Seek like him, and like him you shall obtain it. And Oh ! let those who have obtained it be full of joy. " Praise the Lord, for he is good, for his mercy endureth for ever ;" and as an evidence of having obtained mercy from God, show mercy to men. " Be ye therefore merciful, as your Father also is merciful."

SERMON V.

THE PRODIGAL SON, OR THE PENITENT JOYFULLY RECEIVED

Luke xv. 24. For this my son was dead, and is alive again ; he was lost, and is found. And they began to be merry.

JESUS CHRIST came into the world to save sinners ; he therefore behaved in a kind and affable manner to all, even to some who had been very great sinners. This offended the Jews, and especially the self-righteous Pharisees. They thought that a holy prophet should have nothing to do with such bad people ; not considering that he went among them on purpose to save them from their sins. But Jesus Christ vindicates his conduct, by appealing to the custom of men in general, who always rejoice when they recover any valuable thing that was lost. In this beautiful and affecting parable, we have,

I. The Prodigal's sin and folly, in departing from his father, and living in a riotous manner

II. His repentance and return.

III. His kind reception.

I. We have the prodigal's sin and folly, v. 11—13. " A certain man had two sons : and the younger of them said to his father, Father, give me the portion of goods that falleth to me : and he divided unto them his living. And not many days after, the younger son gathered all together, and took his journey into a far country, and there wasted his substance with riotous living."

The prodigal son is an emblem of a sinner. He disliked the restraint of his pious father. He wanted to be his own master, to live in a state of independence, and to be governed by his own corrupt judgment. The language of sinners is, " Let us break his bands asunder, and cast away his cords from us ;" they say unto God, " Depart from us ; for we desire not the knowledge of thy ways. What is the Almighty, that we should serve him? and what profit should we have, if we pray unto him?" Job xxi. 15. All natural men are, like the prodigal, men of the world, and want their portion in this life, regardless of a portion in heaven : and, like him, they wish to live at a distance from God, and, as much as possible, "without God in the world."

But let us stop a moment, and ask whether this is not a picture of ourselves. Has not each of us, more or less, acted the same part? Is there not in us, even in us, an evil heart of unbelief, in departing from the living God? Is not this the reason that so many forsake the house of God, even on the Lord's day—that they dislike to hear God speak to them in his preached word—that they refuse to speak to God in their prayers—and that they despise truly religious persons, who are of the family of God? Surely all this arises from hearts "alienated from this life of God;" this is "the carnal mind," which is enmity against him.

Observe, now, how he behaves in the distant country to which he went. Probably he told his father that he would traffic with his money, and so mend his fortune; or at least, that he would travel for the improvement of his mind; but he no sooner gets his portion into his hands, and becomes his own master, than he enters upon a loose, lewd, riotous way of life, in the company of bad women and other wicked companions. Thus he *wasted* his substance, and abused the gifts of God; gave himself up to luxury and lasciviousness, "to work all uncleanness with greediness."

See the consequence of being left to ourselves; the misery of departing from God! and Oh, beware of wasting his gifts! Our reason, our health, our strength, our time, our money, our influence, are all talents committed to our trust; let them be used to promote the glory of God, and the salvation of our souls, and not abused to the purpose of sin and destruction.

8 *

Mark now, my friends, how certainly misery follows sin. Ver. 14. When he had spent all, there arose a mighty famine in that land, and he began to be in want. Here is a proof of the truth of that old proverb—"Wilful waste makes woful want." See how the pleasures of sense perish in the using: for "as the crackling of thorns under a pot, so is the laughter of a fool;" a noisy blaze, succeeded by a dismal darkness. Let this, as Solomon advises, "keep thee from the evil woman; from the flattery of the tongue of a strange woman; for by means of a whorish woman a man is brought to a piece of bread. She hath cast down many wounded. Her house is the way to hell, going down to the chambers of death." Prov. vi. 24. and vii. 26.

What was become of the prodigal's gay friends? Would none who had feasted at his table come forward to supply his wants? No: they all deserted him. Place no dependence on sinful companions. Many adore the rising sun, who turn their backs upon it when it sets. And how just it is, that he, who acts as an enemy to God, should not be able to find a friend among men!

One should have thought that now, in his adversity, he would have turned his thoughts homeward. Surely this was a proper time for serious reflection. But he was not sufficiently humbled; rather than to go back to his father, he will submit to the most servile state. Ver. 15. " He went and joined himself to a citizen of that country, and he sent him into his fields to feed swine." It is no disgrace in this country to be a servant, or to feed any sort of cattle: but you are to observe that he was a Jew, and as swine's flesh was forbidden to the Jews, there could be nothing more odious and abominable to him than the care of swine. It seems, too, that this gay youth was a poor, worthless creature, and notwithstanding his education, fit for no better employment. Oh, how are the mighty fallen, and how is the fine gentleman degraded!

But far greater is the disgrace of sinful men. Created at first in the image of God; honourable and happy in communion with him; see him now fallen from his high estate, become a servant of sin, yea, a slave of the devil; a companion of beasts; yea, himself, as Bishop Hall speaks, "Half a beast and half a devil!" Whatever sinners may think of themselves, their wretched business is no other than the prodigal's; they are " making provision for the flesh, to fulfil the lusts thereof," and that is no better than feeding, greedy, dirty, noisy, swine.

Disgraceful as his employment was, could he have got wholesome, though plain food, he might have made himself content. But, to fill up the measure of his misery, we find he was almost starved to death. Having, perhaps, a bad-hearted master, and that in time of famine, he had not a morsel of bread : he must not only feed the swine, but feed with them, and eat the same food. Ver. 16. " He would fain have filled his belly with the husks which the swine did eat"—wild chestnuts, probably, or some such trash, not fit for a man to eat; but though he would have been glad of them, he could not get them, or not enough of them, to satisfy his hunger.

Here also is a picture for the sinner. Husks are food for swine, not for men ; so the things of this world are not more fit to satisfy the immortal soul, than husks to feed the body. They suit not our nature, nor satisfy our desires.

> " Why seek ye that which is not bread,
>   Nor can your hungry souls sustain ?
> On ashes, husks, and air, you feed ;
>   Ye spend your little all in vain."

II. Let us now proceed to a more pleasing part of the subject. " It is a long lane, they say, which has no turning," and yet, alas ! thousands go on all their days in the way to eternal ruin ! But here we have an instance of a sinner, reduced to the last extremity, to whom his afflictions were sanctified, beginning to repent, and return to

God. Ver. 17. "And when he came to himself, he said, How many hired servants of my father's have bread enough and to spare, and I perish with hunger !"

"He came to himself"—remarkable expression ! He had been *beside himself*; he had acted the part of a madman ; and indeed "the hearts of the sons of men are full of evil, and madness is in their heart." Eccles. ix. 3. Do madmen mistake their own condition, and fancy themselves kings and emperors ? so do poor sinners; they think themselves spiritually "rich and increased with goods, &c., and know not that they are wretched, and miserable, and poor, and blind, and naked." Madmen are often desperately mischievous, and even self-murderers. So are all sinners. What madness can be equal to the eternal destruction of the soul for the sake of a few momentary pleasures ? Yes, we are all far from ourselves, when we are far from God ; and we never return to ourselves, till God, in mercy, return to us. Regard not then the foolish reproach of the world, who will say, when you are truly concerned for your souls, that you are mad. No ; *they* are the madmen who live in sin ; *you*, who are coming to God, have come to yourselves.

The Prodigal compares his own wretched state with the condition of his father's meanest servants. "I am starving ; they are feasting. I am miserable ; they are happy." Just so, a repenting sinner plainly perceives his own miserable case, and longs to partake of their happiness, who live in the house of God, and are his devoted servants. "I perish," said he ; so may every man say who lives in sin, "I perish ; but there are others (Oh that I were one of them !) who dwell in the house of the Lord, feast upon his rich grace, know that their sins are pardoned, and are full of peace and joy in believing."

What is the natural consequence of such a comparison ? Why an effort, an immediate effort, to mend his condition. Hope springs up in his heart ; and though there was but a may-be, a mere peradventure of success, he makes the following wise resolution; ver. 18, 19. "I will arise, and go to my father, and will say unto him, Father, I have sinned against heaven, and before thee, and am no more worthy to be called thy son; make me as one of thy hired servants."

He resolves to return to his father. Now, what is conversion, but the sinner's return to God? This is what God calls us to in his word—"Let the wicked forsake his way, and the unrighteous man his thoughts; and let him return unto the Lord, and he will have mercy upon him; and to our God, for he will abundantly pardon." Isa. lv. 7. But with what spirit will he return? Will he feign an excuse, and go with a lie in his mouth? Will he say, "I have been very unfortunate; I have been robbed of my property; been deceived by swindlers; or had a shipwreck at sea?" Or, will he plead his youth and indiscretion, and say, "Though I have done wrong, I had a *good heart?*" Such, my friends, are the wretched excuses of unhumbled sinners. But the Prodigal now perceived the plague of his own heart; he was "poor in spirit;" he would make no excuses; but own his guilt, and confess he was unworthy to be treated as a son; he would be contented and thankful to be admitted into the kitchen or the scullery. "Make me as one of thy hired servants." Thus it will be with every true penitent; he will give glory to God, by making full confession of his sin, and will sincerely admit that he is totally unworthy of the mercy and grace of God."

Observe; he says, "I have sinned *against heaven*"—against the God of heaven: against the high authority of God, and against the wonderful goodness of God. It is a foolish and hurtful mistake of some people, when they speak of a drunkard, or some other wicked man, to say—"He hurts none but himself." It is true, sinners hurt themselves; but they also offend and provoke the God of heaven; and in true repentance, the sinner, like the Prodigal, and like the psalmist, will say, "Against thee, thee only, have I sinned, and done this evil in thy sight." *Before thee,* said he; the Prodigal had sinned against his father, by throwing off his easy yoke : and let young people remember, that disobedient and undutiful behaviour to their parents is a sin against God, that needs his pardoning mercy, and must be repented of.

Shall we pause a moment—and ask ourselves, whether we find in *our* hearts a disposition like that of the Prodigal? We have all *sinned* with him, but which of us *repents* with him? Depend upon it, we shall not think of returning to God, till we feel the misery of departing from him. We have forsaken God, we have set up for our own guides, we have abused the gift of God, we have been the slaves of sin; and have we not found emptiness, insufficiency, dissatisfaction, misery, and danger in this condition? If not, may God open our eyes, and help us to discover it. If we are convinced of these things, let us make the Prodigal's resolution, "I will arise;" and not only make it, but execute it; for we read, ver. 19, *He arose and came to his father.* There are many good resolutions formed, which come to nothing. It has been said, that "the way to hell is paved with good resolutions:" perhaps there is not one unhappy creature there, who did not at one time or other say, "I will arise and go to my father;" but their resolutions died away. The Prodigal, however, arose, and began his journey—a long journey—for you will remember that he went into "a far country." Ah! who can tell what painful fears and doubts assaulted his mind in the way? Hunger had brought him very low; and he might have said, "How can these trembling limbs carry me so many miles? I must beg my way; perhaps I may die on the road : and, oh! if I live to reach the place, how can I bear the sight of the house? My father, my offended father, will refuse to see me, forbid me the house, and after all my labour, I may be rejected, and justly too. But, however, though I may perish if I go, I *must* perish if I stay 'I will arise and go to my father.'"—He goes. He continues his journey; and, at length, after many a weary step, and many a toilsome day, he catches a glimpse of the mansion; he halts; his heart beats: a thousand fears rush into his mind. Ah! what shall I do? What shall I say?

Just then, for so Providence ordered it, "when he was yet a great way off, his father saw him, and had compassion, and ran, and fell on his neck, and kissed him." This is the

IIId. thing we are to consider; his kind reception. God's eyes are upon all his creatures. " He looketh upon men," to see if there be any that regard, any that return; and the very first motions of the heart toward him are noticed. "He looketh upon men; and if any say, I have sinned, and perverted that which was right, and it profited me not; he will deliver his soul from going down into the pit, and his life shall see the light." Job xxxiii. 28.

He had compassion. A parent can readily conceive what tender feelings would be excited by the sight of a long-lost child returning in this miserable plight; and by these feelings the God of mercy is pleased to express his perfect readiness to receive and forgive a repenting sinner.

He ran. The Prodigal, perhaps, stopped short, afraid to venture on; but the father runs; forgetting his age, and the gravity of his character, he runs to meet him, impatient to embrace him.

He fell on his neck and kissed him; though ragged, though filthy, though lately come from feeding swine. Any other than a father would have loathed; but the parent loves, and manifests his love by his affectionate embraces.

What a wonderful display is this of the love of God! It is thus that God presents us with the blessings of his goodness. It is thus that repenting sinners are welcomed by the God of mercy. Hear it, O my friends, hear it for your encouragement, that our God is "ready to pardon, gracious and merciful, slow to anger, and of great kindness."

CONCLUSION.—Men and brethren: There are two things in this parable which I trust you will not forget—*the folly of sinners*, and *the compassion of God.* Let each one of us consider, whether he has not ungratefully run away from God—disliked his restraints—been wise in his own conceit—indulged forbidden lusts—and abused the bounties of heaven. And yet perhaps totally insensible of the evil of so base conduct. In the midst of prosperity there was not a thought of returning to God; and even in affliction trying any other method rather than that. But surely it is high time to bethink ourselves. May divine grace bring us all to ourselves, as the necessary means of bringing us to God. Let us resolve, without a moment's delay, to humble ourselves at his feet; and let us be encouraged to do so, by the affecting account we have heard of God's kindness. "He sees afar off the returning sinners; he pities, he meets, he pardons, he embraces them. He arrays them with the robe of the Redeemer's righteousness; adorns them with the ornaments of sanctifying grace; honours them with the tokens of adopting love; and invests them with all the privileges of his dear children." Oh that we may feel the charming force of these heavenly attractions! May there be joy in heaven and earth this day on our account! and may we, thus received into the house of God, abide there all the days of our life, admiring and adoring the sovereign, free, and everlasting grace of God: and saying, "Behold! what manner of love the Father hath bestowed upon us, that we should be called the sons of God."

SERMON VI.

CHRIST THE WAY TO GOD AND HEAVEN.

John xiv. 6.—I am the way.

IF we believe there is a future state of happiness, called heaven, and a future state of misery, called hell there can be nothing of greater consequence to us, than that we may obtain the one, and escape the other. If we have any serious thoughts of these things, we cannot but inquire, Which is the true way to heaven? Everything that calls itself *Religion*, pretends to be the way; but, as there are so many different ways, they cannot all be right: yea, we are bold to say they are all wrong, except one, and that one is declared in the text; "I am the way, said Jesus; no man cometh to the Father, but by me." Our Lord spake these words to his disciples when they were full of trouble, because he was about to leave them. He comforts them by saying he was going to heaven, his Father's house, to prepare a place for them, and that he would come again, and receive them to himself, that where he was they also might be; and then he adds, "Whither I go ye know, and the *way* ye know." But Thomas, who was rather of a doubting turn of mind, replied—Lord, after all thou hast said, we are still at a loss about the place where thou art going, and how then can we know the way to follow thee? Jesus answered, *I am the way;* which is as if he had said, I am the Mediator between God and man; I am the means of intercourse between heaven and earth; whatever comes from God to a sinner, comes through me; and whatever, of an acceptable kind, goes from a sinful man to God, must pass through my hands. In treating upon these very important and useful words, we shall show—

I. To what Christ is a way; and

II. What sort of a way he is.

9

I. We are to consider, What Christ is a way to. Every way or road leads from some place to another; now, as he is pleased to call himself *a way*, in condescension to our mean capacities, we are to consider what he is the way *from*, and what he is the way *to*. We are to remember that we are fallen, guilty creatures, in a state of sin, and liable to all miseries here and hereafter; and that we are far from God, from righteousness, and from heaven; now, if ever we are brought back to God and a state of grace here, and to a state of glory hereafter, it must be in and through Jesus Christ alone. We say, then, that Christ is the way to God, and the way to heaven.

The first of these is directly expressed by our blessed Lord in the text : " I am the way, no man cometh to the Father but by me." When man was first created, he lived in a happy state of nearness to God; he knew God, and delighted in him as his chief good; but sin, cursed sin, soon made a dreadful separation; and now we come into the world " estranged from God, and go astray from the womb;" we desire absence from God; " he is not in all our thoughts;" but we seek happiness in sin and folly. Yet is the Lord our God pleased to invite us back to him, by the promises and blessings of his gospel, and by the ordinances of his house. And although multitudes despise these, and madly resolve to pursue the way of destruction, yet a happy few there are, who hear the voice of the Son of God in his word, are made sensible, that, being far from him, they must perish, and that it is good for them to draw nigh to him. But these persons have oftentimes such an awful view of the glorious and dreadful majesty of God, as an infinitely holy and just being, and of the distance that sin has occasioned, that they know not how to approach him. The prophet Micah thus expresses the anxious desires of such an one, chap. vi. 6. " Wherewith shall I come before the Lord, and bow myself before the high God? Shall I come be-

fore him with burnt-offerings, with calves of a year old?
Will the Lord be pleased with thousands of rams, or with
ten thousands of rivers of oil? Shall I give my first-born
for my transgression, the fruit of my body for the sin of
my soul?" Blessed be the Lord, "he hath showed us
what is good!" He hath given us a full answer to these
inquiries in our text. Jesus is the way. It is not by
costly offerings of blood or oil, nor at the dreadful expense of sacrificing a darling child; but Jesus is the way.
He not only came to *show* us the way, but *to be* the way.
He did not come to tell us how we may "make our peace
with God," as some express themselves, but to be our
peace; for "he made peace through the blood of his
cross." It is by the death of Jesus that we draw near to
God; so Peter tells us, "He suffered for our sins, the
just for the unjust, that he might *bring us to God.*"
We are far from him; we had neither the will nor the
power to return; and sin, if not atoned for, must have
made an everlasting separation between a holy God and
vile sinners; but Jesus, who was perfectly just and righteous, endured the most shameful and painful sufferings
upon the cross for us, that is, in our room and stead, that
he might reconcile us to God, and bring us to a holy conformity to him, and happy communion with him here,
and to the eternal enjoyment of him hereafter.

In this way, that is, in Jesus, we have free access to
the glorious Majesty of heaven; we may, by prayer in
his name, "come with boldness to the throne of grace,"
there to "obtain mercy, and find grace to help us."
Hear what Paul says of this matter, Heb. x. 19, &c.
"Having, therefore, boldness to enter into the holiest by
the blood of Jesus, by a new and living way which he
hath consecrated for us, through the vail, that is to say,
his flesh, let us draw near with a true heart, in full assurance of faith." What a glorious privilege is this! We
may approach the great God, as our reconciled God and
Father; we may use holy freedom with him in our

prayers; we have this liberty of access by the merit of Christ's blood, and by the application of it to our consciences through faith therein. This is the way prepared for our use, even Jesus, who is " the way, the truth, and the life;" he is the truth and substance of all the ordinances of the Old Testament; with particular reference to the rending of that vail which separated the holy of holies in the temple from the holy place; and which rending took place at the moment of our Saviour's death; which signified that now the way to God and heaven is laid open for all believers; and that is the second thing proposed.

2. Jesus Christ is the way to heaven. This indeed follows the other; for if we come to God by Jesus as our reconciled Father, if sin be pardoned, and we are admitted to a life of holy communion with him here, it is certain that we shall also have " an abundant entrance into his heavenly kingdom and glory." Jesus died, to " redeem us *to God*," to his favour and image here, and to his glory hereafter. He died, to " bring many sons to glory;" that they may be satisfied with the goodness of his house; even to his holy temple, that they may be pillars in that temple, never more to go out; that they may approach him in a more sublime way of worship than at present, without the help of means and ordinances; that they may " see him face to face," without a cloud to hide his glory from them, and without the clog of sinful flesh and blood. Now Jesus is the only way to heaven. This is the record of the gospel—" God has given to us eternal life, and *this life is in his Son*." There it is, and nowhere else: and whoever thinks to get to heaven another way, misses the true road, and will be eternally disappointed. There are many ways to hell, but only one to heaven; and if *Jesus* be not our way, we shall never get thither. As sinners, we have forfeited heaven and deserved hell; but Jesus Christ has not only redeemed his people from the curse, that they may not go

to hell, but by his perfect obedience or righteousness he has procured for them *a title to heaven.* The righteousness of Christ is " to, and upon, all who believe in him;" it is imputed to them, or reckoned to their account, as if they had themselves performed it; and on this ground it is that they are admitted into the realms of light and glory; " *therefore* are they before the throne, because they have washed their robes, and made them white in the blood of the Lamb;" and not on account of any goodness, virtue, or good works of their own.

II. Show what sort of a way Christ is.

1. It is a *living* way. This way to heaven was by Christ's *dying;* yet it is called a living way, because all our life springs from his death. Christ is the life of all who live spiritually or eternally. This way is trodden only by such. All who are in this way are alive to God, and, what is more, they shall never die. The eternal life of all who are in Christ, and walk in him, is secure; for because he lives, they shall live also. No man ever died upon this road. "I am," saith Christ, " the resurrection and the life ; he that believeth in me, though he were dead, yet shall he live; and whosoever liveth and believeth in me shall never die." The body indeed must die, because of sin, though that is more properly called *sleep,* in the New Testament, and the body shall be raised in glory; " but the spirit is life, because of righteousness," and shall never perish, but have everlasting life.

2. It is a *plain* way. Some ways are hard to find; have many turnings and windings and cross-paths; but this way is easy to find, and to keep. The prophet Isaiah, speaking of it, says, " The wayfaring men, though fools, shall not err therein." Isa. xxxv. 8. It is an infinite mercy, that the things which belong to our peace are not difficult. There are, it is true, deep and difficult things in the Bible; but the grand truths which concern our salvation are perfectly plain and easy. What can be

9 *

plainer than what is said about our fallen, sinful, helpless
state, as sinners? or about Jesus Christ, as the only all-
sufficient Saviour? or about our duty, as saved sinners,
towards God as man? It is a great blessing to poor
people, that these things are so plain, and that God by
his Spirit makes them so, even to " babes and sucklings;"
for " the entrance of his words giveth light : it giveth
understanding to the simple."

3. It is a *free* way. There are *private* ways that belong to great men, and they are open to few; it would be
a trespass for a stranger to be found in them; but this is
a *public* way, the king's *high-way*. Paul says, it is con-
secrated, that is, appointed, dedicated, devoted to this
purpose, and free for the use of all who desire to travel
in it. There are no bars or toll-gates, where travellers
must pay for permission to enter or proceed; for salvation
is " without money and without price" Isa. lv. 1. It
is a way prepared on purpose for the use of *sinners*, who
are returning to God; and no objections are made to
such persons. No worthiness, nor qualifications, nor con-
ditions, are required of the traveller; whosoever will,
may come and welcome. It is a free way.

4. It is a *safe* and *sure* way. It is a firm solid road,
there is no danger of sinking in it, for Christ is the rock
of ages. It suffers no alterations by rains and floods, as
other ways do; it is passable at all times; there is
nothing at any time to hinder our access to God, and pro-
gress to heaven. Nor is there any occasion to fear enemies upon it. There are such; but they cannot prevail.
" The devil (says one) has been busy upon this road for
about five thousand years, but never yet slew one believer;
for every traveller is 'kept by the power of God, through
faith, to salvation.'" So that he may walk on with boldness, and fear no evil; rejoicing to think that every believer, that once set his foot in this way, has been enabled
to proceed, and not one of them failed of " receiving the
end of his faith, even the salvation of his soul."

5. It is a *pleasant* way. The scripture says, "The ways of wisdom are pleasantness, and all her paths are peace." Satan invites men to travel in the ways of sin, under the notion of their being pleasant; and there certainly are pleasures in sin; but they are for a short season; they are now mingled with bitter pains and pangs of conscience, and they will issue in misery everlasting. But "the ransomed of the Lord," who return to the heavenly Zion, "shall come with songs and everlasting joy upon their heads." Believers are called upon to "rejoice always in the Lord." Those who travel in this way are not only secure from harm, as you have heard, but the Lord has engaged for their supply on the road; he has promised that "they shall be abundantly satisfied with the fatness of his house, and drink of the rivers of his pleasure." They shall "sit under his shadow with great delight, and his fruit be sweet to their taste." They shall enjoy the company of the saints as their fellow-travellers, with whom their communion shall be sweet. Yea, the Lord of the way himself has promised to bear them company, and has said, "Fear not, for I am with thee;" and "I will never leave nor forsake thee."

Lastly, it is the *only* way. Many ways to God and heaven have been proposed by mistaken men, under the influence of the great deceiver, the devil: and it is too commonly supposed that *any way* will do, if a man is but sincere in it. But this cannot be true; for if any way of man's invention might suffice, what occasion was there for Christ to come from heaven, obey the law, and endure the curse, that he might become our way? For, "if righteousness come by the law," or men can be their own Saviours, or partake of the mercy of God without an atonement, all the vast expense of Christ's sufferings and death might have been spared; yea, in that case "the grace of God is set aside, and Christ is dead in vain." Gal. ii. 21. But Christ crucified is the only way; so Peter solemnly declares, Acts iv. 12. "Neither is there salvation in any other, for there is no other name under heaven, given among men, whereby we must be saved. There is salvation in his name ; it was procured by him, and he ever lives to bestow it; it is also published by divine authority; it is given forth in the preached gospel; but there is no other, *under heaven*, given for that purpose; none given by God's orders; if any others are given, it is by impostors and deceivers. Jesus only is the way to God and heaven. Thus you see that Christ is a *new* way—a *living* way—a *free* way—a *safe* way—a *pleasant* way, and the *only* way.

SERMON VII.

THE VAIN EXCUSES OF SINNERS EXPOSED.

Luke xiv. 18.—And they all, with one consent, began to make excuse.

THE blessings of the gospel in Christ are, in the parable of which the text is a part, fitly compared to the dainties of a noble and costly feast. " A certain man made a great supper, and bade many," ver. 16. So Christ has made plentiful provisions in his gospel for the souls of men, and freely invites all who hear it to be partakers " And he sent his servants at supper-time, to say to them that were bidden, Come, for all things are now ready," ver. 17. So Christ having called the *Jews* by his own ministry, sent the apostles after his resurrection to renew the invitation, and to say that the work of redemption was finished, and that he was willing to receive all who should come by faith to him ; and this is the language of the gospel wherever it is preached.

If we consider the nature of a feast, we shall see how properly our Saviour compares the blessings of our salvation to it. In a feast we expect *wholesome provisions*

—*plenty*—*variety*—*elegance*—*company, and the* whole *gratis.* All these, and more, Jesus gives us in his gospel. Here is "*the bread of life* which came down from heaven," without which we must for ever perish; but eating which secures our eternal life. Here is *plenty*, for in our Father's house there is bread enough and to spare; and however many the guests who come, still "there is room." Here is *variety;* pardon, peace, holi- ness, adoption, joy in the Holy Ghost, communion with God, perseverance to the end, and glory, to crown the whole. Here is *elegance;* dainties worthy God to be- stow; dainties fetched from heaven; dainties purchased at a cost beyond the value of a thousand worlds—for " Christ's flesh is meat indeed, and his blood is drink in- deed !" Here is *good company;* for, sitting down at the gospel feast, " we come to an innumerable company of angels; to the general assembly and church of the first- born ; and to God, the Judge of all; and to the spirits of just men made perfect; and to Jesus." And, what is best of all, it is *gratis*—" without money, and without price"—" the poorer the wretch, the welcomer here."

We shall first notice the three excuses which follow our text ; and then proceed to mention other excuses and objections which are often made.

1. " The first said—I have bought a piece of ground, and I must needs go and see it; I pray thee have me ex- cused."

This is the plea of a *rich* man, who had been adding field to field. He was under no kind of necessity to view the land he had bought : probably he had seen it before he had bought it; if not, he might have stayed till another day, and have found the field in the same condition ; but he wanted to feast his eyes upon his new purchase. See here an instance of the inordinate love of the world, the pride of possession, the deceitfulness of riches. This was a man of the world, whose portion was in this life," for the sake of which he was deaf to the call of Christ. Oh, how hardly shall they who are rich enter into the kingdom of heaven ! so great is the danger of loving the world too much.

2. "And another said—I have bought five yoke of oxen, and I go to prove them : I pray thee have me excused." Here is the man of *business :* the former was taken up with pleasure ; this with care. "Too much leisure, or too much business, are equally dangerous to the soul." This was a frivolous excuse like the former ; another day would have done as well for proving oxen in the plow, for the purchase was already made ; but anxiety for the world prevailed over his spiritual interest. And what is this but the common excuse of tradesmen, labourers, and women who have families ? *I have no time to spare for religion.* Let me ask you, What is your time for ? Is not the care of the soul *the one thing needful?* Should you not seek *first* the kingdom of God and his righteousness ? Besides, " what will it profit, if you gain the whole world, and lose your own soul ?" And let me tell you, there is time enough to mind the affairs of both worlds, and both are best minded together : the one need not shut out the other. Religion will not make men idle ; it will make an idle man industrious ; it tends even to worldly prosperity. " Godliness is profitable for all things, having the promise of this life, and of that which is to come."

3. The excuse of a third person was, " I have married a wife, and therefore cannot come." Here is an excuse of another kind, which takes in too great a regard to creatures, and too much fondness for domestic enjoyments, and the pleasures of this life. It was a very weak excuse ; for though he had married a wife, he might surely have left her for a few hours, without a breach of proper affection ; or he might have taken her with him to such a great feast as this, where so many were bidden, and none forbidden ; or he might have gone alone, if he could not persuade her to go with him. How

many perish by the unlawful use of lawful things, and undue regard to carnal relations!

All these excuses were, as you see, frivolous and foolish; they were all of a worldly kind; and indeed it is *the world*, in some form or other, that proves the great hindrance of men's salvation. But there are many other excuses, which people are apt to make, equally absurd. I shall proceed to notice some of them.

4. Some object, and say, *Your religious people are hypocrites; after all their pretences, they are like other folks.* I answer by a question—Are they *all* hypocrites? If so, there is no such thing as religion in the world; if so, the Bible is all a lie, and Christ must have shed his blood in vain; for he died to redeem us from the world, and our vain conversation in it, and to make us a holy people zealous of good works. It is admitted there are some hypocrites; and woe be to them! There was a hypocrite, a Judas, even among the apostles; but religion did not cease because of him. If there was not a reality and an excellency in religion, there would be no hypocrites; if guineas and bank-notes were not valuable, there would be no counterfeits; and, I presume, you do not refuse to take any money, because there is base coin; nor would you excuse yourself from paying your rent to your landlord, because you are afraid of taking bad money. If there are hypocrites, as you say, and we allow, then there is the greater need to look to yourself, that you are sincere; but I greatly doubt the sincerity of those who make this excuse; and their hearts tell them it will not be admitted at the bar of God. Besides, it is censorious and wicked to judge another man, and to call him a hypocrite, unless his life is bad; but, because you can find no blemish in the life of a truly religious person, you presume to search his heart, and call him a hypocrite. The truth is, you would be glad to prove him such, as an excuse for your own want of religion.

5. Methinks I hear another person say—*I see no oc-*

casion-to make so much fuss about religion.—You say truly; *you* do not see : but your not seeing is a proof of nothing but your own blindness; a blind man sees nothing. If you examine the word of God, you will find the christian life compared to a warfare; now a soldier's life, in the time of actual service, is not idle. It is also compared to a race, in which great exertion and activity are necessary, if a man would so run as to obtain the prize. A christian is represented in scripture as " crucifying the old man of sin," and " mortifying the deeds of the flesh ;" and can these things be done by the slothful man, who is a stranger to zeal himself, and hates to see it in another? Has not God required you to love him with all your heart, and all your soul, and all your mind, and all your strength; and do you know anybody that does more than this? Let me also ask you, Why is it that you commend industry in worldly business, and despise it in religion? If there be a hell to avoid, and a heaven to obtain, and sin to destroy, and a God to serve, and a soul to save—why should you not be as earnest in religion as you are in the world? Why should not a christian love God as much as you love money, or sin? I know the answer your heart makes.

6. Another cries—*I shall do as well as my neighbour: and if I perish, God help thousands!* I reply, If you do not better than the thousands that perish, God help you! Jesus Christ has said, " Wide is the gate, and broad is the way, that leadeth to destruction, and many there be which go in thereat ;" while the narrow way to life is found and trod by few. Think not well of your state, because you are like others : you have greater cause to suspect it. Christ's flock is small; but the devil's herd is large. " The whole world," says John, " lieth in wickedness." Follow not, then, the multitude to do evil, but consider their end, and be wise. It is a very affecting and useful story that Mr. Baxter relates in his " Call to the Unconverted." " I remember," says he, " a

circumstance that a gentleman told me he saw upon Acham-bridge, over the Severn, near Shrewsbury. A man was driving a flock of fat lambs; and something meeting them, and hindering their passage, one of the lambs leaped on the walls of the bridge, and his legs slipping from under him, he fell into the stream: the rest, seeing him, did, one after one, leap over the bridge into the stream, and were all, or almost all, drowned. Those that were behind did little know what was become of them that were gone before, but thought they might venture to follow their companions; but as soon as ever they were over the wall, and falling headlong, the case was altered. Even so it is with unconverted carnal men. One dieth by them, and drops into hell, and another follows the same way; and yet they will go after them, because they think not whither they are gone. Oh! but when death hath once opened their eyes, and they see what is on the other side of the wall, even in another world, then what would they give to be where they were?"

7. Perhaps another person will say—*It is true I am a sinner bad enough; but I do some good things, and will not they atone for my sins?* Paul shall answer. "Without shedding of blood there is no remission;" the good works of men were never appointed to the office of a Saviour; for "if righteousness come by the law, Christ is dead in vain." Why do we call Jesus a *Saviour*, and yet hope to be saved by our works? which is to become our own Saviour. But the word of God has settled this, and declares, Eph. ii. 8, "By grace are we saved, through faith; and that not of ourselves, it is the gift of God; not of works, lest any man should boast." And to say the truth, no man can do works good in the sight of God until he is first justified by faith, for even "the prayers of the wicked are an abomination to him;" and the thirteenth Article of the Church of England truly says, that "Works done-before the grace of Christ, and the

inspiration of his Spirit, are not pleasant to God; and we doubt not but they have the nature of sin."

8. Unwilling to humble himself, and cry for mercy, another says—*I am no scholar, and God expects no more than he gives.* I answer, You may be a true christian, and yet no scholar. God has sent you his word, and you can *hear* it, if you cannot read it; not to say, that since Sunday-schools have been set up, every person almost may learn to read, if he will. But know this, my friends, that ignorance will excuse none. Where knowledge is a duty, ignorance is a sin. It is not your want of opportunity to know the gospel, but your want of inclination to it, that keeps you ignorant. You take pains to know how you may get food and raiment, or charity; why then remain contentedly ignorant of "the things which belong to your everlasting peace?" Isa. xxvii. 11. 2 Thess. i. 8.

9. Another person, advanced in years, says—*I am too old to change my religion.* What do you call religion? Is it a set of notions and ceremonies? Is it an attachment to certain ministers and buildings? This is not religion. Religion is the devotedness of the heart to God; and without this the most pompous forms are of no avail. Nicodemus was an old man when he came to Christ, who said to him as we say to you, "Except a man be born again he cannot see the kingdom of God." In a word, if your religion has not changed you, it is high time to change your religion.

10. Methinks I hear another say,—*I intend to be better at some future time.* So did Felix, who trembled when Paul preached, and said to him, "When I have a convenient season, I will call for thee;" but that season never came. The way to hell is paved with good intentions. Should you die in your sins, which God forbid! out of your own mouth will you be condemned; for you are forced to admit that all is not right; and yet you venture to go on in sin, though you know not what a day may bring forth.

Go to the sick and dying bed of a neighbour, and hear him groan and complain of an aching head and sick stomach; observe his shaking hand and disordered pulse; the rattling throat, the convulsed limbs, and the cold sweat; and say, is this a time for repentance? Are these poor dregs of life all you should offer to God? Oh! be wiser; nor leave the service of God, or the salvation of your soul, to so improper a season.

But, after all, the true reason remains untold. May not all your excuses be summed up in this one?—*I love sin, and cannot part with it;* but observe, you must part with sin, or part with heaven. You must turn or burn. And are you content to enjoy the present pleasures of sin for a moment, and endure everlasting pains, which are their certain consequence? It is related of a man, who, by his excesses, was in danger of losing his sight; and being told by the physician that he must change his course or lose his sight, replied, " Then farewell dear light !" Thus many, by persisting in sin, seem to say, —Farewell God of mercy, Saviour of sinners, Spirit of holiness ! farewell ye people of God! farewell life of happiness, heaven, and glory! and, for the sake of dear sin, welcome devils, welcome darkness, despair, and misery, for evermore.

APPLICATION.—Thus, we have taken notice of some of those excuses which sinners often make, who love darkness rather than light; who follow lying vanities, and forsake their own mercies. But it is plain that all these excuses arise from the darkness, worldliness, and enmity of our fallen nature, and they show the necessity of having " a new heart, and a right spirit." These excuses will scarcely now satisfy those who make them ; they will miserably fail them in the prospect of death; and they cannot be accepted at the bar of God. In the parable before us, it is said, that " when the servant showed his Lord these things, *he was angry,* and said, None of those men which were bidden shall taste of my supper." God forbid this sentence should go forth against any person here. As yet, our gracious Lord commands us to " go out into the high-ways and hedges, and compel them to come in, that his house may be filled." In his name we come, and call you to the gospel-feast. Knowing the terrors of the Lord, we persuade you; and knowing the bounty of the Lord, we invite you. None ever repented of coming; nor were any rejected who came. Come then to Jesus. "The Spirit and the Bride say, Come; and let him that heareth, say, Come; and let him that is athirst, come: and whosoever will, let him take of the water of life freely."

> All things are ready, come away,
> Nor weak excuses frame;
> Crowd to your places at the feast,
> And bless the founder's name."

SERMON VIII.

THE VALUE OF THE SOUL.

Matt. xvi. 26. For what is a man profited, if he shall gain the whole world, and lose his own soul? or what shall a man give in exchange for his soul?

TO give these words their full force, remember whose they are. They are the words of Jesus Christ, the incarnate God, the Creator of the world. And who so able to determine that the soul is worth more than the world, as he who made them both? He made the soul, and he made the world; yea, the price he paid for the redemption of the soul was his own precious blood. Surely then he knew the value of the soul. Regard these words, my friends, as full of truth, and truth of the greatest importance to yourselves. And oh that he who first spake them to his disciples, may now speak them to our hearts by his Holy Spirit!

In the text there are three things which require our attention :

I. Every man has a soul of the greatest value.

II. There is a possibility of a man's losing his soul, yea, great danger of it.

III. The whole world can make no amends for the loss of the soul.

I. Every man has a soul of the greatest value.

The nature of the human soul is, at present, but imperfectly known. God has not told us so much about it, as to gratify our curiosity; but enough to assist our faith. From the scriptures alone we learn anything satisfactory concerning our souls; and there we find that the soul is a something distinct from the body; a thinking immortal substance ; and capable of living separately from the body in another world. This appears from Matt. x. 28, where our Lord says to his disciples—"Fear not them which kill the body; but are not able to kill the soul; but rather fear him, which is able to destroy both soul and body in hell." In like manner, we learn from the parable of Dives and Lazarus, that the soul of the former was tormented in hell, while his body lay buried in earth. Jesus Christ assured the penitent thief on the cross, that he should be with him that very day in paradise, while, as we know, the body of Jesus was laid in the tomb. It is said of Judas, *that he went to his own place*, which certainly was hell ; but his wretched carcass was on earth. Paul declared, that death would be *gain* to him, because, when *absent from the body*, he should be *present with the Lord ;* useful as he was in the church, and happy in that usefulness, he rather desired to die, to depart, *to be with Christ*, which was far better.

Now this immortal soul is of immense value: and its excellency may be argued from the following considerations :

10 *

1. Its *origin;* it came immediately from God. Something peculiar is said of the formation of man, Gen. i. 26. "God said, Let us make man in our image after our likeness." Surely it was the soul of man, rather than his earthly body, that bore the divine resemblance.

2. Consider again the vast and noble *powers* of the soul. When these powers are assisted by learning, how does the philosopher survey, measure, and describe the heavenly bodies, or search into the hidden secrets of nature !

3. Once more, consider the worth of the soul in the amazing *price* paid down for its *redemption* "Forasmuch as ye know that ye were not redeemed with corruptible things, as silver or gold ; but with the precious blood of Christ, 1 Pet. i. 18, 19. Thousands of rams, or ten thousands of rivers of oil, would not have sufficed : nothing but the blood of the Lamb of God could atone for sin.

Surely the ransom price of the soul bespeaks its infinite value. Oh ! let us learn to value our souls !

4. Consider again, the *contention of heaven and hell* for the soul of man. Heaven from above invites us to come to God. Jesus Christ came down on purpose to show us the way ; yea, to be himself the way. The ministers of the gospel " watch for souls ;" for this they study and pray, and travel and labour, that they may snatch perishing souls from the devouring flames. They are " instant in season and out of season," and are " all things to all men," that they may win some. Your serious relations, friends, and neighbours, long for your conversion ; for this purpose they pray for you, speak to you, and lend you books. Yea, the angels of God are waiting around us, longing to be the messengers of good news to heaven, that sinners are repenting on earth.

On the other hand, it is the business of the devil to tempt and destroy the souls of men. As a subtle serpent he lies in wait to deceive, or as a roaring lion he roams about to destroy. Gladly would he seduce you into sin by the love of pleasure, or get you to neglect salvation by the love of business, or prejudice your minds against the gospel of life.

5. Above all, consider the immense value of the soul, in that vast *eternity* of bliss or woe that awaits it. We are but in an embryo state at present, like a bird in the egg, or an infant in the womb. We shall soon die into eternity. We shall soon begin a state of being that will never end. The present life is merely the seed-time of eternity, and "what a man soweth that also shall he reap; he that soweth iniquity shall reap vanity"—he shall meet with nothing but disappointment. "He that soweth to the flesh shall reap corruption; but he that soweth to the spirit shall reap life everlasting." Gal. vi. 20. Considering the endless duration of a soul, the happiness or misery of one saved or damned sinner will be far greater than the temporal happiness or misery of all the inhabitants of the earth for a hundred years.

II. That a man may lose his soul, and that he is in danger of so doing.

The soul of a man cannot be lost by *ceasing to be :* for, being immortal in its nature, that is impossible. And oh! how gladly would a damned soul cease to be, if it were possible ! But for a soul to be lost is, for it to be lost to that happiness, here and hereafter, which is suited to its nature. It is to lose all the present pleasures of religion, " the consolation that is in Christ," " the comfort of love," the " peace that passeth all understanding," and " the joy of the Holy Ghost, which is unspeakable and full of glory."

But, oh ! who can tell the fearful import of that word *lost*, as it respects the future and eternal world ? The following is related of a boy, who was sent upon some errand on a cold winter's evening, was overtaken by a dreadful storm, when the snow fell so thick, and drifted in such a manner, that he missed his way ; and, continuing several hours in that condition, was ready to perish. About midnight, a gentleman in the neighbourhood thought he heard a sound, but could not distinguish what it was, till, opening his window, he heard a human voice, at a great distance, pronouncing in a piteous tone—*Lost! lost! lost!* The poor boy, in some hope of help, kept crying out at intervals, *Lost! lost! lost!* Humanity led the gentleman to send persons diligently to seek for the lad, who was at length found and preserved. Happy for him that he perceived his danger, that he cried for help, and that his cry was heard! So will it be happy for us, if, sensible of the value of our souls, and their danger of perishing in hell, we now cry for mercy and help to that dear and gracious " friend of sinners," that great and generous deliverer, who " came to seek and to save that which was *lost.*"

Now, would we escape this dreadful end? Let us, then, seriously consider the danger of losing our souls. That there is danger of doing so, the word of God abundantly declares. Remember what Christ himself said, " Enter ye in at the strait gate; for wide is the gate, and broad is the way, that leads to destruction, and many there be who go in thereat." Is there no danger then? Mark again what is said by the psalmist. " The wicked shall be turned into hell, and all the nations that forget God." The word of God describes the very people. See a list of them in 1 Cor. vi. 9, and mark, whether any of you are there described. " Know ye not that the unrighteous shall not inherit the kingdom of God? be not deceived; neither fornicators—nor adulterers—nor effeminate;" that is, persons of lascivious tempers and practices, however private and alone—" nor sodomites—nor thieves—nor covetous—nor drunkards—nor revilers—nor extortioners, shall inherit the kingdom of God." Look over this black catalogue again, and if you find your name there, own it. Blush and tremble to think what it must be to be shut out from the kingdom of God, and so lose your own soul; and then say, is it worth while to lose your soul for any of these sinful pleasures and practices? Will you, with your eyes open, exchange your soul for any of these things?

I find, again, that all *impenitent* persons—all *unconverted* persons—all *unregenerate* persons, and all *neglecters of the gospel*, will lose their own souls; and that you may be sure of this, I will mention the chapter and verse where it is so declared. All *impenitent* people, Luke xiii. 3. "Except ye repent, ye shall all likewise perish."—All *unconverted* people, Matt. xviii. 3. "Verily I say unto you, Except ye be converted, ye shall not enter the kingdom of heaven."—All *unregenerate* people, John iii. 3. "Verily, verily, I say unto thee, Except a man be born again, he cannot see the kingdom of God."

Thus it is plain, that the soul may be lost, and that there is great danger of it. Why else did the Son of God come down from heaven? Why has he sent his gospel to us? Why else do the ministers of Christ cry aloud and spare not? Why else do they warn every man, and teach every man, but that they may convince sinners of their danger, and prevent them from losing their own souls? We now proceed to show,

III. That the whole world can make no amends for the loss of a soul.

"What is a man profited, if he shall gain the whole world, and lose his own soul?" It is not here supposed, that it is in the power of any man to conquer or possess the whole world. No man ever yet *saw* all the world, and life would be too short for that purpose. But it is to gain all the riches, honours, delights, and pleasures, that a man can possibly enjoy. It is to have every idea accomplished, every sense gratified. It is to have the lust of the flesh, the lust of the eye, and the pride of life indulged in the highest perfection. All that can please the palate; the luxuries of all countries collected on the table of the epicure; all the delightful charms of music;

all the elegancies and conveniences of a noble palace;
all that can gratify the smell and the touch; all the pleasures of imagination, arising from grandeur, beauty, and
novelty;—and, supposing all this obtained—Solomon obtained it all.   And what a *poor all* it proved! " Vanity
and vexation of spirit" was the total amount.

And is this the whole of that for which men risk their
souls?   Foolish barter!   Wretched exchange!   Was
Esau wise, who sold his birthright for a mess of pottage?
Was *Judas* wise, who sold his master, and his own soul
too, for thirty pieces of silver?   Just as wise as the
worldly man, who parts with heaven for the sordid and
short-lived pleasures of earth.   I remember reading of a
woman, whose house was on fire.   She was very active in
removing her goods, but forgot her child, who was sleeping in the cradle.   At length she remembered the babe,
and ran with earnest desire to save it.   But it is now too
late.   The flames forbade her entrance.   Judge of her
agony of mind, when she exclaimed, " O my child, my
child! I have saved my goods, but lost my child!"   Just
so it will be with many a poor sinner, who was all his life
" careful and troubled about many things," while "the
one thing needful" was forgot.   What will it then avail
for a man to say—" I got a good place, or a good trade,
but lost my soul!   I got a large fortune, but lost my
soul.   I got many friends, but God is my enemy. I lived
in pleasure, but now pain is my everlasting portion.   I
clothed my body gaily, but my soul is naked before God."
Our Lord exposed this folly in the parable of the worldly
rich man, Luke xii. 16, &c.   His wealth increased abundantly.   He was about to enlarge his barns.   And then
he promised himself a long life of idleness, luxury, and
mirth.   " But God said to him, Thou fool, this night
shall thy soul be required of thee : then whose shall those
things be which thou hast provided ?"

Here, for the sake of the body, the soul was forgot.
While he was dreaming of years to come, death was at

the door; and little did he think, "that the next hour his friends would be scrambling for his estate, the worms for his body, and devils for his soul."

APPLICATION.—But why should you lose your souls? Is there not a Saviour, and a great one? He came from heaven on purpose to save that which was lost. Do you ask, "What shall I do to be saved?" We reply with the apostle Paul, "Believe in the Lord Jesus Christ, and thou shalt be saved." There is no name under heaven given among men whereby we must be saved, but that of Jesus. He is the only deliverer from the wrath to come. Take care that you trust in nothing else. Make not your good works, as they are called, your dependence. Virtue and morality are excellent things, and promote the peace and welfare of society, but they are not saviours. He that trusts them leans on a broken reed, builds on the yielding sand, and will be wofully disappointed at last. By *grace* alone are sinners saved, through *faith;* and faith is the gift of God. Many, who have some concern for their souls, perish through their ignorance of Christ. They think themselves moral and devout, and doubt not that God will accept them. But this is a ruinous mistake. Such moral persons are in as much danger as the most profane. This is the fatal stumbling-block of thousands. But know this, Christ alone can save our souls. He must be your wisdom, your righteousness, your sanctification, and redemption; your all in all. Fly then to him without delay. If you would not lose your soul, call upon him to save it. This is his office: he is the SAVIOUR. It is his delight: he waits to be gracious. His open arms are ready to receive the trembling sinner. Turn ye to the strong hold, ye prisoners of hope. Believe in him, and you are safe. You may then say, with Paul, "I know whom I have believed, and am persuaded that he is able to keep that which I have committed to him," namely, the immortal soul, with all its eternal concerns, *against that day,* the day of final judgment.

SERMON IX.

THE PENITENT THIEF.

Luke xxiii. 42, 43.—And he said unto Jesus, Lord, remember me when thou comest into thy kingdom. And he said unto him, Verily I say unto thee, To-day shalt thou be with me in Paradise.

WHO can read these words, or consider the conversion and pardon of the dying thief, without exclaiming, in the words of Paul—" Where sin abounded, grace did much more abound ?" Here is a wonderful instance of divine, free, and sovereign grace, abounding towards the chief of sinners. It is recorded for the encouragement of great sinners, in every age, that *they* may take refuge in Christ " who are ready to perish ;" and it affords a pleasing proof that " he is able to save *to the uttermost*, all who come to God by him."

Our blessed Lord was crucified with two thieves, and placed between them, that he might be thought the worst of the three. But thus the scripture was fulfilled, " He was numbered with the transgressors," or " criminals." The chief priests, the scribes, the rulers, and the mob, all joined in mocking and deriding him ; not content with beholding his extreme sufferings, they had the cruelty to add insult to his pains. " Come down from the cross," said they, " and then we will believe. Thou that didst save others, save thyself :" and " Save us too," said the thieves ; not seriously, but by way of taunt ; for, it is written, " the thieves also, which were crucified with him, cast the same in his teeth." Oh what an instance is this of the savage hardness of the human heart ! how dreadful, that wicked men, dying in their sins, should strive to forget their own agonies, that they might join in abusing and insulting the Son of God ! A state of more desperate and confirmed wickedness can hardly be conceived.

But behold the grace of God! One of these men is snatched as a brand from the fire : plucked, as in an instant, out of the very jaws of destruction. An astonishing, perhaps a sudden change is produced. He cries for mercy, and he obtains it. He looks to Jesus, and is saved. From being a hardened sinner, he becomes at once an eminent saint; obtains assurance of immediate bliss; and passes from the cross to glory.

Let us now carefully consider the two parts of our text, into which it naturally divides itself.

I. The prayer of the dying malefactor.

II. The gracious answer of the Saviour.

In attending to the first, consider, for a moment, the character of the criminal, for a criminal he was; a malefactor; a highwayman : one who belonged to a desperate gang of robbers who infested that country; a set of seditious banditti, who were for shaking off the Roman yoke, and who lived by rapine and plunder. It is not improbable that he was a murderer also; for such men scruple not to kill as well as steal. This is the man who becomes the trophy of sovereign grace. For surely it will be admitted that here was no previous goodness or worthiness to recommend him to the divine favour.

Is it not astonishing to hear such a man as this suing for mercy? But what cannot grace effect, and that in a moment? He who in the first creation said, "Let there be light, and light there was," can, in an instant, dart a ray of spiritual light into the darkest mind.

Behold he prayeth! So it was observed of Saul, as a proof of his conversion. So we say, with wonder and surprise, of the thief—Behold he prayeth! Perhaps he never prayed before, or he had long forgot to pray. Had he prayed, he had not come to the cross; he had not been a thief : for, according to the Dutch proverb, "Praying will make a man leave off sinning, or sinning will make a man leave off praying." Now he prays; and, most wonderful! prays to Him who hung upon a cross. He becomes

11

a christian at once, for a christian is one who " with the heart believeth unto righteousness, and with the mouth maketh confession (of that faith) unto salvation." Rom. x. 10.

He calls Jesus, LORD, which no man can do aright " but by the Holy Ghost." He gives him this title of dignity and authority, though degraded by the whole Jewish nation, and branded with the name of a rebel, a Samaritan, an impostor.

He owns him also as a *King*, for he begs to be remembered by Jesus, " when he shall come into his *kingdom*."

He pays him the just honour of having heaven at his disposal, according to what our Lord afterwards declared, " I am he that liveth and was dead ; and, behold, I am alive for evermore, and have the keys of hell," or, rather, *the unseen world*, including both heaven and hell. Rev. i. 18. The dying thief believed this, and his prayer was the language of faith, a confidential address to the Saviour.

Observe also the *modesty* of his application. *Remember* me ; not *prefer* me to honour in thy kingdom, as the two ambitious disciples had formerly requested ; but, simply, *remember me ;* he does not dictate how, or in what manner ; he leaves it all to the Lord ; but he commits his cause, his soul, to Christ ; and, no doubt, with some degree of that satisfaction, which Paul expressed in the view of death ; " I know whom I have believed, and am persuaded that he is able to keep that which I have committed unto him against that day." 2 Tim. i. 12. It was a request like that which Joseph made to the butler, Gen. xl. 14, " *Think on me*, when it shall be well with thee ; yet did not the chief butler remember Joseph, but forgot him." The poor thief succeeded better ; he was remembered, and saved ; for Jesus never said to any soul, " Seek me in vain." " Whosoever shall call on the name of the Lord shall be saved."

As the case of this man was singular and extraordinary,

so he gave very singular and extraordinary proofs of his sincerity. The professions of repentance and faith, first made in the hour of distress and in the prospect of death, are often uncertain, and may justly be suspected. Too many who, in the expectation of death, have seemed to be much in earnest, and gave great hope to christian friends of a real change, have proved by their conduct, when they recovered, that they were not sincere ; for the vilest of men generally respect religion in their dying hours. But the penitent thief was enabled to give the most satisfactory evidence of sincerity ; and the answer of Christ to him puts it beyond a doubt. Observe now the marks of his sincerity.

1. *He reproves sin* in his comrade, especially his sin in reviling Christ—" Dost thou not fear God, seeing thou art in the same condemnation ?" Persecutors of Christ, in his person, or in his members, awfully prove their want of the fear of God : and every sin is greatly aggravated by that hardness of heart which persists in it, even in the time of sore affliction. True repentance will always occasion a sincere hatred to sin. True grace will ever make a man feel for others. The love of God and the love of man are always united. The true penitent will say with penitent David, " Then will I teach transgressors thy ways, and sinners shall be converted unto thee." Ps. li. 13.

2. *He condemns himself*, and admits the justice of God and of the magistrate in bringing him to the fatal tree—"We suffer justly, for we receive the due reward of our deeds." Shameful and painful as our death is, it is no more than we deserve. A just sense of sin will make a sufferer patient. He will say, " Against thee, thee only, have I sinned, and done this evil in thy sight ; that thou mightest be justified when thou speakest, and clear when thou judgest." Ps. ii. 4.

3. *He vindicates Christ*—" But this man hath done nothing amiss." The Jewish courts had condemned him

to death as the vilest of miscreants, and the whole multitude had cried, " Crucify him, crucify him;" but the thief, more honest and better taught than they, justifies his whole character: and truly says, " he hath done nothing amiss." Thus, in the face of all his infamous and powerful slanderers, he declares the innocence of Jesus, who was, indeed, " holy, harmless, undefiled, and separate from sinners."

Thus was clearly manifested the reality of that great and gracious change which had taken place in his heart. He was evidently enlightened in the knowledge of Christ; he was convinced of his sin and misery; he was humbled for it; he reproved sin in his neighbour; he honoured the character of Christ; he owned him as Lord, and King, and Saviour; and he commits his departing spirit into his faithful hands. What wonders of grace were crowded into this small space, enabling him, in a few minutes, to give more glory to Christ than many do in the whole course of their lives !

II. Let us now proceed to consider the gracious answer of our Saviour to his dying request. " And Jesus said unto him, Verily I say unto thee, To-day shalt thou be with me in Paradise."

How readily does God regard the sinner's cry ! With speed like that which winged the feet of the Prodigal's aged father, who no sooner beheld at a distance his long-lost, but now returning son, but " while he was yet a great way off, had compassion, and ran and fell upon his neck, and kissed him." God is slow to anger, and quick to mercy ; ready to forgive. He discerns the first motion of the soul heaven-ward, and while the sinner is " yet speaking" in prayer, the prayer is heard and answered.

Observe the substance of the answer—a place in paradise—Christ's company there— immediately, " to-day ;" and the solemn assurance of the whole, " Verily, I say unto thee," it shall be so.

A place in paradise is promised ; a place in hell was

his desert, and would have been his portion, had he died in the same state he was in half an hour before. Heaven is here called "Paradise;" in allusion to the garden of Eden which the Lord God himself planted, and in which he put the man he formed. By sin, Adam soon lost his garden, and his God. "He drove out the man." By the first Adam, Paradise is lost; by the second Adam, the Lord from heaven, Paradise is regained; a far better Paradise; a garden from whence the blessed inhabitants shall never be driven out. "Here grows the Rose of Sharon, and the Lily of the valley. Here flourishes the plant of renown; here the unforbidden tree of knowledge, and the unguarded tree of life." No subtle serpent annoys this happy spot, any more to seduce; nor shall the free will of man betray him to ruin again.

Jesus promises to the penitent the enjoyment of *his own company there*—" this day thou shalt be *with me* in Paradise." Christ, then, was going, not to hell, to redeem the damned, as some have supposed, but to heaven; where he assures the thief he shall also be. It is the presence of Christ that makes heaven so glorious and happy. With this he consoled his mourning friends, John xiv. "I am going to prepare a place for you; and I will come again, and receive you to myself, that where I am there ye may be also." Amazing favour, " to be with Christ !" this is enough. He asked a bare remembrance, as if distant; Jesus promises his own immediate presence.

And how quickly was this to be enjoyed! "To-day." He had prayed—"Lord, remember me when thou comest into thy kingdom." He knew not when that might be; perhaps he thought of some very distant time. Christ says " to-day." How short and speedy was this man's journey to glory ! In the morning, he was posting to hell; in the evening he is with Christ in heaven. This scripture teaches us a pleasant truth, namely, that there is no interval between the time of our departure from this

11 *

world, by death, and our admission into the realms of glory. Some have dreamed that the soul sleeps till the resurrection; but Christ assures the thief, and assures us by the same word, of an immediate entrance into heaven; that so, being " absent from the body," we may be " present with the Lord."

APPLICATION.—Beware of abusing this glorious instance of free grace. Many have been very cautious in speaking of it, and have rather laboured to obscure its glory, by studying to find out something good in the character of the thief, lest this example of grace, purely free, and granted at the last hour, should have a dangerous tendency, and encourage men to defer their repentance; presumptuously hoping to be saved at the last moment, like the thief. But a sober consideration of the matter may prevent this abuse; while we must take care to do nothing to diminish the glory of divine grace, in this instance so illustriously displayed. It has been often and justly observed, " We have but *one* such instance recorded in all the Bible: *one* sinner converted at the hour of death, that we may hope; and *but* one, that we may fear." And suppose it had once happened that a person had leaped down from a lofty precipice without losing his life, would it be prudent for ten thousand other people to run the risk, and leap down after him? Dreadfully hazardous, indeed, it is, for men to presume on a death-bed repentance. " Repentance is the gift of God;" he is bound to bestow it at no time; and can it be reasonably expected at the close of a life of sin and rebellion? Let it be considered how many die suddenly, without a moment's warning; how many die on their beds, who are so flattered by their disorder, or their friends, that they have no expectation at all of death. Others die in the delirium of a fever; or are otherwise disabled by extreme agony or weakness for serious reflection. And some die hardened, like the other thief on the cross; for, in general, men die as they live.

May the goodness of God, so divinely displayed in this instance, draw thee to repentance.   Jesus Christ " came, to seek and to save that which was lost."   This was always his character, and he maintained it to the last. His enemies reproached him for it; they called him " the friend of sinners;" so he was ; but not the friend of sin. Blessed be his name, he is " the same yesterday, to-day, and for ever," he casts out none that come.   Oh ! come, and try him.   What encouragement is here for him " that is ready to perish ;" who has a world of guilt, and not a grain of worthiness !   Say, with the dying thief, " Lord, remember me, now thou art in thy kingdom," and he will find a place in Paradise for you, even for you.

SERMON X.

IRRESOLUTION REPROVED, AND DECISION RECOM- MENDED.

1 Kings xviii. 21.   And Elijah came unto all the people, and said, How long halt ye between two opinions?   If the Lord be God, follow him ; but if Baal, then follow him.

IN various periods of human life, and particularly in youth, there is a remarkable hesitation as to the choice a person shall make.   On the one hand religion demands his attention ; sets before him the destructive consequences of sin, and the necessity of forsaking it ; requires him to relinquish the bewitching vanities of the world, and offers him, in their stead, the pleasures of a good conscience, and an eternal weight of glory in the future world.   But nearer at hand, the smiling world presents her flattering joys ; invites him immediately to taste her delights, and leave both the bitters and sweets of re- ligion to another day.

Are there any here who thus hesitate ?—I have a mes-

sage from God unto you : the message which Elijah delivered to the tribes of Israel on the most solemn occasion,
when hesitating whether to worship Jehovah or Baal.
" How long halt ye between two opinions? If Jehovah
be the true God, let him alone be worshipped : but if
Baal can prove his divinity, let him have your adoration."
Why hesitate any longer? If the religion of Jesus be
true, and holy, and good, why neglect to be seriously religious? If the way of sin and folly be safe and right;
if God and conscience approve; and you are sure that it
will end well—then pursue it without reserve."

Favour me with your serious attention to what I shall
offer upon the two following observations .

1. Many persons, and young persons especially, are irresolute and changeable with respect to religion.

2. Such is the reality, pleasure, and advantage of true
religion, that it deserves and demands our whole hearts ;
and we ought not to hesitate a moment about giving them
fully to it.

Let us first observe, (and who has not observed it?)
that many persons seem to hesitate, and show that they
are irresolute and undetermined, whether they shall be
religious or not.

In this state the person resembles king Agrippa, who,
under the temporary impression of Paul's preaching, was
constrained to say—" Almost thou persuadest me to be a
christian"—almost! alas! *only* almost, not altogether
persuaded; some secret reserve is yet made; the strong-
hold of the heart is yet in the possession of sin, which,
without the interposition of almighty grace, will ere long
regain all its former dominion.

The bewitching pleasures of sin once. more begin to
court the soul: some youthful lusts present their flattering baits to the senses, and find within a party eager to
catch at them. We are fallen creatures; our minds are
become carnal; and we have a strong propensity to indulge the flesh. The seed of every sin is deposited in

our corrupt nature; and though the seed may long continue dormant, yet, if, like a vegetable seed that has been buried deep in the earth, it be brought towards the surface, and placed in a favourable situation, it will unfold all its hidden powers, and ripen into open transgression. Such is the fascinating power of sin, especially when become habitual, that it will insist upon indulgence at any rate; even at the expense of fortune, character, and life itself. And now all those promising appearances before spoken of disappear, and are covered, like the writing on the sea-shore, with the overwhelming tide.

The strong attraction of evil company is another source of danger. Man is formed for society; and we may add, he is formed *by* his society, whether it be good or evil. When Satan sinned and fell, he speedily drew man into the same condemnation. When Eve was prevailed upon to taste the forbidden fruit, she hasted to induce her husband to commit the same transgression. It is observable, what pains are usually taken by the votaries of pleasure and of vice, to lead their companions into the same; how strongly do they solicit the young and the unsuspecting, to become parties in their ensnaring amusements and dangerous pleasures! Not content with their own sin and ruin, they become the missionaries of Satan, and labour to make proselytes for hell. But oh, that the advice of the wise man were regarded—" My son, if sinners entice thee, consent thou not!"

The fear of shame, on account of religion, keeps many in a hesitating state. Glorious and highly honourable as the religion of Jesus certainly is, the advocates of sin will pretend that it is a mean and low thing, not fit for persons of discernment, of taste, of fashion; they will say, that to be moved with religious affections, is to be irrational and enthusiastic; and that your religious people, with all their pretensions, are only concealed hypocrites, and all their devotion merely whining and cant. Here, perhaps, the youth is brought to a stand. " Shall I then," says he, "encounter all this shame and disgrace? Must I, if religious, be treated with contempt by the world in general? Who can endure this?"

But stop, my friend, and let us argue this matter. What do you blush at? Are you ashamed of acknowledging your Creator, and bowing the knee before your Redeemer? Is it an unreasonable thing to credit the God of truth, or to love him who is infinitely amiable? Is it mean and base to secure your everlasting happiness, even while at the same time you are promoting your best interests upon earth? If you are tempted to yield to the world, because it forms the great majority, you are in a mistake. "There are more, far more with us than with them." I know that the visible crowd of deceived mortals take part against religion, but what are they, compared with those who espouse it? Is not the great and eternal God with us? Does not he approve the humble and the pious soul? Is not Jesus, the glorious Saviour, with us? He was once himself despised and rejected of men on account of his piety, and now he is exalted on the throne of glory, he knows how to pity and defend his persecuted people. On our side we boast the innumerable tribes of angels, whose business and delight it is to minister to the heirs of salvation. Shall we be ashamed to do the will of God on earth as angels do in heaven?

Thus then we see the tempted soul halting between two opinions. At one time, religion appears not only necessary, but excellent and beautiful: the Sabbath a sweet day of devotional rest; the house of God has a thousand charms to invite attendance; the Bible a book of sacred instruction and entertainment; and prayer, a rational and delightful employment. But, through the power of temptation, at another time, the scene is changed. Insensibly mixing with men of the world, the heart is seduced again, and gayety, music, dress and dancing assume new charms and captivate the affections.

Then religion sinks in the scale. Religion seems to wear a frowning aspect; the cavils of the infidel gather weight and importance; and infidelity promises, not future happiness, but present gratification, and that without the restraints which were feared before. Religion offers to make the man a saint; but as this appears too laborious, he relinquishes the future hope, and inclines to become a happy brute.

But still the mind is unsettled. Conscience is on the Lord's side. Something within yet withholds assent, and fears that all will not end well at last. The very sight of a good man will shake its confidence. A tolling bell, the view of a funeral, the news of a sudden death, or the apprehension of a fit of sickness, will excite alarm : and a faithful sermon will make the man like Felix tremble. How many have we known, who, when spectators of the death of others, or under apprehensions of their own, have found their ground untenable, and have admitted that there is a reality in religion, and that it is necessary to their peace .

2. Such is the reality, pleasure, and advantage of true religion, that it deserves and demands our whole hearts.

But you will say, What do you mean by religion ? The question is good. I will answer it. I mean by religion, not a system of opinions, nor a set of ceremonies; but a humbling conviction of our ruined state by sin; the application of the soul to Christ, as an all-sufficient Saviour; and a sincere endeavour to oppose sin and live unto holiness. This is real religion—the religion of the gospel— the religion which the Holy Spirit teacheth, and the disciple of Jesus learneth. It is for the mind to be enlightened, so as to discover the holy character of God; to see our own deformity in the glass of his holy law; to be humbled in the dust as penitent sinners : and then heartily to embrace the salvation proclaimed by the gospel; to receive Jesus as our teacher, our righteousness, and our Lord, and to give up ourselves, without reserve, to be his for ever.

This religion is a glorious reality. It is scriptural; it is rational; it is experimental; it is practical. It answers the true ends of religion; it makes us holy and happy. It renews the heart; it reforms the manners; and secures eternal bliss.

This is the religion, which, for substance, has been the choice and the practice of all the wise and good men who ever lived, from the days of Abel until now. This is the religion we affirm to be very pleasant and advantageous; for it includes the sublime delight of a good conscience delivered from guilt by the atoning blood of Christ; the inexpressible pleasure of communion with God in his ordinances, public and private; the privilege of society with the excellent on earth; preservation from a thousand mischiefs and miseries to which the irreligious are liable. It affords a solid ground of consolation in the unavoidable evils of life; and it sustains the soul amidst the awful circumstances of death, with a lively hope full of immortality.

These and many more are the *present* advantages of true godliness: but who can describe those which are to come? Who can tell what are the joys at God's right hand—what it is to be with Christ, and behold his glory —what it is to enter into the joy of the Lord; to see him as he is; to be partakers of the inheritance of the saints in light; to spend eternal ages in the beatific presence of God and the Lamb?

" Choose then, this day," this moment, " whom you will serve. If it seem evil unto you to serve the Lord; choose this day whom ye will serve." Only remember, " ye cannot serve two masters." God will not accept of a divided heart. Does your heart say—" God forbid that we should forsake the Lord?" Then be it so. From this happy moment, let it be a settled point, religion, serious religion, vital religion shall be my first great business, and everything that opposes it shall give place. So say, and so do, my brethren, and you are made for ever.

Shall I then add, as Joshua in a similar case, "Ye are witnesses against yourselves, that ye have chosen you the Lord to serve him. And they said, We are witnesses?" May God confirm your resolution, and by his almighty grace ever enable you to act conformably to it!

SERMON XI.

CHRIST THE GREAT PHYSICIAN.

Matt. ix. 12. But when he heard that, he said unto them, They that be whole need not a physician, but they that are sick.

IT is obvious to all, that a man in perfect health, who feels no pain, and is conscious of no disease, will not employ a physician. Whatever reports he may have heard respecting him, or whatever opinion he may entertain of his skill, he sees no present occasion for his assistance; and this was the condition of the Pharisees while our Lord was upon earth. He came "to seek and to save that which was lost;" and in the pursuit of this benevolent object, he disdained not freely to converse with publicans and sinners: not that he meant to countenance their sins; no; he mingled with them only to reclaim them, just as physicians go among the diseased merely to effect their cure. But this gave great offence to the proud Pharisees—men "who trusted in themselves that they were righteous, and despised others." They complained of his conduct to his disciples, saying, "Your master keeps company, and eats and drinks with publicans and sinners;" but "Wisdom is justified of her children." Our Lord, in the text, vindicates his own conduct, while he accounts for that of the Pharisees: "The whole need not a physician, but they that are sick."—

12

These men are insensible of the state of their own souls, while others were rejoicing that they had found a remedy.

These words may teach us the four following things:

First—That sin is the disease of the soul.

Secondly—Jesus is the great physician.

Thirdly—Those who are insensible of their sins, neglect him.

Fourthly—Those who know their true condition, are very desirous of his help.

In the first place, we are taught that sin is the disease of the soul. We brought it into the world with us, deriving it from our first parents; for "by one man sin entered into the world, and death by sin." It is with strict propriety that sin is thus described, for it has just the same effects upon the soul that disease has upon the body. Sickness destroys all our powers of action, and deprives us of ability to transact our affairs, however important and urgent they may be: whatever dangers we might avoid, whatever advantages we might obtain, there is a total inability for action; and thus it is with the soul. We have before us a vast eternity, and this is the only season for preparation; it is the seed time of eternity; we are now called upon to "work out our own salvation with fear and trembling;" but while this sickness prevails, we have no heart to engage in this great work; we cannot bear the thought of necessary exertion. Even the ordinary means of grace are frequently neglected; the Bible, and prayer, and Sabbaths, and sermons, are shunned; for the sinner has no heart to them.

Sickness deprives a man of rest; he cannot be composed; he feels a constant uneasiness, an insatiable thirst: and thus, as the scripture saith, "There is no peace to the wicked;" he turns from creature to creature, seeking rest and finding none; the world disappoints him; he meets with repeated and perpetual difficulties; this perhaps irritates his temper, and makes him a burden to himself and others; to get rid of his cares, he flies to amusements and intemperance; but the disease, instead of being relieved, is aggravated, and he grows worse and worse.

Disease frequently occasions delirium. A sick man knows not where he is, or what he says; when he is at death's door he fancies himself perfectly well, and if not prevented, would be in danger of destroying himself. Thus a man in a state of sin is furiously bent on his own ruin; he will not be persuaded there is any danger in his case; and he is very angry with the servants of Christ who would convince him of his error. Solomon says, "The heart of the sons of men is fully set to do evil; madness is in their hearts while they live, and after that they go to the dead." How do such persons fondly imagine that their hearts are good, even while their ways are perverse and desperately wicked!

Sin deforms the body. "When God with rebukes correcteth man for his iniquity, he maketh his beauty to consume like a moth;"—"He changeth his countenance, and sendeth him away." The finest face may be soon disfigured, and the most lovely person become loathsome; but, in the sight of God, nothing is so beautiful as holiness, nothing so loathsome as sin.

Finally, disease is the forerunner of death. Many diseases are mortal in their tendency, and if not seasonably checked, will bring the patient to the grave. Some diseases baffle the skill of the ablest physician. Sin, which is the disease of the soul, is certainly mortal, if Christ the great physician does not interpose: "Death was the original threatening, to keep man from sin." God said to Adam, "In the day that thou eatest" of the forbidden fruit, "thou shalt surely die;" and die he did; his body became mortal; and though he had a long reprieve, he returned at length to the dust from whence he came. But he immediately suffered a moral death; he became "dead in trespasses and sins," and liable to the bitter pains of eternal death. And thus, "by the offence of one, judgment came upon all men to condemnation." This is our state: we are, universally, dead in sin; we have bodies doomed to the grave, and souls exposed to the just anger of an offended God. This is indeed a miserable state; but it would be far more so, if there were no remedy. "Is there then no balm in Gilead; is there no physician there?" Blessed be God, we can, with confidence, say, There is a physician, and he no less a person than the Son of God; and this is what we propose,

In the second place, to notice—That Jesus Christ is the great Physician. There is none upon earth equal to the cure of the souls of men, but the Son of God; he pitied us in our low estate; he saw us perishing in our sins and in our blood; and he left his throne of glory— visited this sinful globe—took our nature into union with his own; yea, he "himself took upon him our infirmities; he hath borne our griefs, and carried our sorrows; yet we did esteem him stricken, smitten of God, and afflicted; but he was wounded for our transgressions; he was bruised for our iniquities; the chastisement of our peace was upon him, and with his stripes we are healed." When on earth he gave many gracious specimens of his power to heal the *souls* of men, by healing their bodies; and such was his power, that "all manner of diseases,"— "every sickness and every disease" among the people was healed; yea, such was the compassion of our blessed Lord, that of all the numerous crowds of sick and afflicted people who applied to him, not one of them was sent away without relief.

In the cure of our souls two things are necessary: we are guilty, and must be justified; we are polluted, and must be sanctified: he performs both these parts of our cure; which is intimated by the expression, that out of his side came water and blood. See the 1st Epistle of John, 5th chapter, and 6th verse, "This is he that came by water and blood, even Jesus Christ; not by water only, but by water and blood." So that this may encourage us to apply to him, and say,

"Be of sin the double cure—
Cleanse us from its guilt and power."

Seeing, then, there is such a great and able Physician, may we not ask, "Why is not the hurt of the daughter of my people healed?" This leads us,

In the third place, to observe that men generally are too insensible of their sins, to apply to Christ; "the whole need not a physician." It is the worst symptom of the disease of sin, that men are totally insensible of it, or think themselves so slightly diseased, that they are in no danger; and, at all events, that the future season will be time enough. Sin destroys all our faculties; it blinds the eyes of our understanding, and deadens the feelings of our hearts; the mind is so darkened, that it does not behold sin as it is, and dreadful mistakes prevail, respecting its true and dangerous nature. Let us endeavour to detect some of these.

Some of these fatal mistakes among men arise from ignorance of the holy law. If sin be "the transgression of the law," we ought to consider, what are the demands of that law; and we shall find it requires perfect obedience to the will of God, and that, flowing from perfect love to him; it requires also that we should love our neighbour, in all instances, as ourselves. Now, while men are ignorant of this holy law, they discover no disease; but when, as in the case of Paul, the commandment comes, with a powerful conviction of its spiritual nature, unsatisfied demands, and fearful curse, then, like him, they are ready to die.

Another mistake respects the depravity of our natures. Of this most men are ignorant. "God made man upright, but he hath sought out many inventions." Man is now an apostate creature, and it may be said of him, in all his faculties, as was said of Israel, in all the branches of her civil and ecclesiastical estate, "the whole head is sick, the whole heart is faint."

Another dangerous mistake respects their opinion of

12 *

their own goodness. How many persons fancy they have good hearts, good desires, good intentions; they mean, they say, no harm, they do none to any man, even while they are living in open rebellion against God, and in the total neglect both of his law and of his gospel. Thus it is that men deceive themselves; they are " whole" in their own esteem, and are angry with those who would convince them of their danger, though with the friendly design of their obtaining a cure. Others will admit that all is not quite right; they cannot say they are in perfect health, but they see no occasion to be alarmed; they are not worse than others : besides, say they, God is very merciful, and he will not deal with his creatures severely; and if they should come short at last, the merits of Christ will make up the deficiency; besides, they design to reform and repent, at some future period. Now all this discovers a dreadful degree of ignorance; they are strangers to themselves, and to the nature of that gospel, which, take it in which view you please, always supposes that man is in a fallen, dangerous situation. And hence it has justly been called " the religion of a sinner;" hence too we find, that men have " followed after the law of righteousness, but they did not attain unto it :" the reason was, " they sought it not by faith, but by the works of the law." Rom. x.

Take a view of the gospel itself for a few moments, and you will see that the gospel supposes the condition of man to be not that of one who is whole, but who is exceedingly diseased. Why is the love of God in giving his Son spoken of as amazing love, as transcending all manner of conception ?—" God so loved the world, that he gave his only-begotten Son;" and for what end? That men " *might not perish*," as they must have done but for this marvellous provision of love, but " that they might have everlasting life." Again the love of *Jesus Christ* is spoken of as the most extraordinary thing in the world, and as absolutely necessary for the salvation of man—that one must die for the people—" the just for the unjust." Our case must have been without remedy, but for him, and his death is represented as being the sole foundation of our hope; so that to depend upon anything else is, in effect, to frustrate the grace, and to say that " Christ died in vain." Again, Take a view of the offices of our dear Redeemer, and what do they imply? Is he a prophet? Then we were ignorant creatures, and needed his instructions. Is he a priest? Then we were guilty, and wanted his sacrifice. Is he a king? Then we were feeble and weak, and unable to defend or rule ourselves. Look at all the operations of the Holy Spirit, and they speak the same language, and while they hold out to us the divine and only remedy, they imply strongly our wretched state. Now all those that are ignorant of this, neglect to apply to the Lord Jesus Christ; but some acquaintance with it is found in all those who resort to him for relief —such as, in our text, are described as " sick." This leads us,

In the fourth place, to observe, that those who know their true condition will gladly apply to Jesus Christ as their physician. For the eyes of their understandings are enlightened; they see the law of God in its spiritual nature and extensive requirements; they perceive the fearful consequences of its violation, for " Cursed is every one that continueth not in all things that are written in the book of the law to do them." Further, their heart is softened, the heart of stone is taken away, and God has given them a feeling heart of flesh; the conscience is quickened; convinced, it may be, at first, of some one particular and flagrant transgression; but they are led back in painful reflection on the whole of their past lives, recollecting long-forgotten sins, and tracing them to the sad source of all—Original Sin. Hence earnest desires and sincere prayers are offered for relief. " What shall I do to be saved?" is the anxious inquiry. " Behold he prayeth !" is the observation that every one makes upon the returning sinner; then, indeed, the soul applies in earnest to the gospel of the grace of Jesus, and the gospel displays his ability to heal; it shows us that Jesus is possessed of almighty power; it shows that he possesses the same power that created and supports the world. The gospel also displays the loving heart of the compassionate Redeemer; it records also the wonderful cures he has already performed, and which are left upon record for this reason, that in all future ages great sinners may be encouraged to repent; then the soul looks up to him as the Israelites looked to the brazen serpent in the wilderness, when stung by the fiery serpents, and ready to die of their wounds; and whoever thus looks to him shall be immediately healed; persuaded, fully persuaded both of his power and his grace, the soul finds health restored, and peace afforded to his guilty conscience.

SERMON XII.

SINNERS ARE SELF-DESTROYERS, BUT SALVATION IS OF GOD.

Hos. xiii. 9.   O Israel, thou hast destroyed thyself, but in me is thine help.

FROM these words I shall show,
First, That sin is a most destructive evil.
Secondly, That every sinner is a self-destroyer.
And thirdly, That there is help and salvation in Jesus Christ, even for self-destroying sinners. "O Israel, thou hast destroyed thyself, but in me is thine help."
In the first place, we shall show that sin is a most destructive evil; and if men were convinced of this, the great point in religion would be gained: but men's persistence in sin, their false peace, and their neglect of the

gospel,—all prove they are *not* convinced of this; and we ourselves, in fact, seem to be but *half* convinced.

To prevent the impression of this awful truth—that sin is a destructive evil—Satan interposes with his first lie. "Ye shall not surely die," said he to our first mother, though God had said, "In the day thou eatest thereof thou shalt *surely* die;" and in the same way, Satan has ever maintained his destructive system; it is by this means, chiefly, that he has "deceived the whole world." We are likewise cautioned against "the deceitfulness of sin;" and we are told that "the heart of man is deceitful above all things, and desperately wicked." Oh, when these three notorious deceivers meet together, woe be to man—a deceitful heart, deceitful sin, and a deceitful devil, aided by the general opinion and practice of a deceitful world in every successive age! Transgressors think it very hard that their beloved pursuits should be deemed so dangerous and destructive; but we appeal to "the law and to the testimony." The same word which assures you that there is a God, that you have an immortal soul, that it is appointed for men to die and come to judgment, that there is a future resurrection, that there is a heaven and a hell,—the same word assures you that sin is a most destructive evil. What was it but sin that destroyed the happiness of angels in heaven, transformed them into infernal demons, and rendered them miserable for ever? What was it that destroyed the happiness of our first parents in the garden of Paradise? Why did God drive them out? What destroyed the image of God in human nature? for man was made in the image of God; but what is he now? an awful mixture of the brute and the fiend. Now we find darkness instead of knowledge, depravity instead of holiness, guilt instead of righteousness.

Turn your eyes to the surface of the earth. What destroyed its original fertility, and made it productive of "thorns and of thistles?" The ground was "cursed for man's sake," because he was a sinner. What has destroyed the general tranquillity of man? It was sin that opened the door to millions of evils. The poor babe enters weeping into the world, while it risks the life of its mother! What legions of fierce and loathsome diseases assail us in every stage of life—in infancy, in youth, and in old age! Behold the youth carried headlong by his tumultuous passions into vice, extravagance, and destruction. See then the man in middle age, struggling with labour, poverty, care, vexation, and disappointment; and then behold age, bending under the weight of infirmities, and saying, "Thou art righteous, O God, but 'thou writest bitter things against me, and makest me to possess the sins of my youth.'"

Sin is the grand disturber of the world. It is sin that disturbs the conscience, that disturbs families, churches, cities, and nations. None will deny that it has destroyed millions of millions of the human race, sweeping away, once in about every thirty years, all its numerous inhabitants, "for dust we are, and to dust we must all return." What vast multitudes die in their infancy! What multitudes are cut off by intemperance! How many have perished by bloody persecutions! and still more by direful wars! What myriads have been drowned in the seas, or consumed by lightning, or swallowed up, by hundreds and thousands at a time, by fearful earthquakes! and oh that this, awful as it is, were the worst! but still further destruction awaits the impenitent, and without an interest in the great salvation of Christ, the *soul* as well as the body must be destroyed—not, indeed, by annihilation, which the wicked would earnestly desire, but by "a second death"—an eternal banishment from the presence of God. Fear him, then, who can not only "kill the body, but who is able to cast both body and soul into hell." Yes, sin is indeed destructive. "The wages of sin is death," and, as James saith, "When lust hath conceived, it bringeth forth sin; and sin, when it is finished,

bringeth forth *death."*   Hear also what the holy law of
God denounces against every transgressor : " Cursed is
every one that continueth not in all things written in the
book of the law to do them."   This then is the state of
the case, and is it not most true that sin is a destructive
evil ?   O Israel, thou hast *destroyed* thyself ! and this
will appear more plainly by showing,

In the second place, that

Sinners are self-destroyers.   " O Israel, thou hast destroyed *thyself."*

What is more shocking than for persons, renouncing
that natural self-love which rules all mankind, to prepare
for their own destruction the fatal bowl, the knife, or the
pistol, or the halter, or to plunge into a watery grave ?
Here we pity, while we blame ; and yet all wilful sinners
are acting the same desperate part ; they are destroying
themselves, and yet they are not aware of it ; and if they
are at all apprehensive of their errors, they are apt to
throw the blame on others, yea, even upon the blessed
God himself.   Against this presumption the apostle
James cautions us, " Let no man say when he is tempted,
I am tempted of God—God tempteth no man ; but every
man is tempted when he is drawn aside of his own lust."
Sinners, although they are self-destroyers, always endeavour to throw off the blame from themselves upon
others.   Our first parent wished to transfer the blame
from himself, and therefore said, " The woman whom
thou gavest to be with me, she gave me of the tree and I
did eat."   She also, as unwilling to bear the blame, said,
" The serpent beguiled me, and I did eat."   Thus also it
is that sinners blame their passions, and charge their
vices upon their constitutions, or upon their companions,
or upon their situations in life, and sometimes upon
Satan ; but unless the tempter had found a proneness in
us to sin, all his temptations would be fruitless, as they
were when they were exercised upon the Lord of life and
glory.   Alas ! all the sins we commit flow from our own

polluted hearts. So our Lord says, in the 15th chapter of the Gospel of Matthew, "Those things which proceed out of the mouth, come forth from the heart, and those are the things which defile the man." It will be found, therefore, that the blame is all our own; that there is an obstinate persistence in sin against the remonstrances of conscience, and the admonitions of God. Thus, of old, he spake unto the house of Israel, "As I live," saith the Lord, "I have no pleasure in the death of the wicked, but that the wicked turn from his way and live. Turn ye, turn ye from your evil ways, for *why will ye die*, O house of Israel?" This expostulation plainly throws the guilt upon man, as his own destroyer; why *will ye die*, O house of Israel?—it arises from the wilful obstinacy and hardness of the human heart. The prophet also charges the Jews with a wilful resistance to the gospel, "they shut their eyes that they might not see; they stopped their ears that they might not hear;" and our blessed Lord says expressly to the unbelieving Jews, " Ye will not come unto me, that ye might have life;" and in our Lord's admirable discourse with Nicodemus, as recorded in the 3d chapter of John, it is expressly said, " He that believeth on him is not condemned, but he that believeth not is condemned already, because he hath not believed in the name of the only-begotten Son of God," and "this is the condemnation, that light is come into the world, and that men have loved darkness rather than light, because their deeds are evil; for every one that doth evil, hateth the light, neither cometh to the light, lest his deeds should be reproved."

True penitents will readily confess this; they will take shame to themselves; and say with the royal penitent, "Against thee, thee only have I sinned, and done evil in thy sight." Yes, real christians, under their deepest afflictions, will adopt this language, " Shall a living man complain,—a man for the punishment of his sins?" And, depend upon it, whatever excuses men now make, the time will come when " every mouth shall be stopped, and all the world be found (and confess themselves) guilty before God." "The books will be opened," and a clear impartial statement made, and the righteous judgment of God will be apparent to all; it will then appear that the way of sin was chosen, that it was preferred, and that wilful unbelief prevailed. Sinners know what frequently passes in their own minds concerning this; they put a force upon themselves, and stifle all convictions; resolving, whatever the consequences may be, that they will proceed. Sinners are self-destroyers—but we go on,

In the third and last place, to show that

There is salvation in Jesus Christ, even for self-destroying sinners.

Oh! what news, what good news, what unexpected news, do we find in this third part of our subject? " O Israel, thou hast destroyed thyself,"—and what might be expected to follow?—You must take the consequences? it is the fruit of your own doings? but, instead of this, God has been graciously pleased to say, " In me is thine help found." Thus, in another place, where we have a long and a black catalogue of the sins of Israel—where the heavens and the earth are called upon to witness their iniquity, yet it is followed up with this encouraging language—" Come now, and let us reason together," saith the Lord, " though your sins be as scarlet, they shall be as white as snow, though they be red like crimson, they shall be as wool."

The help—the salvation which sinners stand in need of, can only come from God. " Shame and confusion of face belong unto us,"—but it is added, (O blessed addition!)—" To the Lord our God belong mercies and forgiveness, though we have rebelled against him." The truth is, man neither wants this help, nor could procure it, if he did. Man does not want it; he sees little or no need of pardon; he justifies his offences, in part, and is inattentive to that gospel which proclaims redemption. And as to another great branch of it, the sanctification of our nature,—he not only does not desire it, but he dreads it; he has no sort of wish for it, and the name of a *Saint* is, in his opinion, nearly the same as that of an hypocrite, or a fanatic.

But if men really desire it, how could they obtain it? Who could have devised that wonderful plan of redemption which is laid before us in the gospel? Who could have made atonement for the sins of the world? Who could have cleansed the foul hearts of men, and made them new? Who could have procured a good title to endless glory? As well might a sinner create a new sun, or a new moon, or a new world, as to bring about the least part of this great salvation. But God says, " In me is thy help found." Mercy, unsought as well as undeserved, first moved his gracious heart : " He remembered us in our low estate, for his mercy endureth for ever." Hence that marvellous, that unparalleled, that unspeakable gift,—God's own dear Son, incarnate in our nature. " Help was laid upon him, who came, not to condemn the world, but that the world through him might be saved. In the 89th Psalm he says, " I have laid help upon one that is mighty, whom I have chosen from among the people." It pleased God to punish the sin of man in the person of his Son. " He was wounded for our transgressions, he was bruised for our iniquities, the chastisement of our peace was upon him, and with his stripes we are healed." " He died, the just for the unjust;" he bore the curse to remove it from us; he was " made sin for us, that we might be made the righteousness of God in him,"—through him there is pardon for sins of the deepest dye. Yes, if any one sinner had as much guilt as usually falls to the lot of a thousand, there is pardon even for such an one, if he come to God through Jesus Christ. In order to encourage the chief of sinners, we find examples held forth, such as that of the apostle Paul in the 1st Epistle to Timothy, i. 15. " This is a faithful saying, and worthy of all acceptation that Christ Jesus came into the world to save sinners, of whom I am the chief; howbeit, for this cause I obtained mercy, that in me first, Jesus Christ might show forth all long-suffering, for a pattern to them which should hereafter believe on him to life everlasting."

Yes; there is sufficient help, for every purpose of our salvation, not only for the pardon of the greatest sinners, but grace that can conquer the most obdurate hearts, even those that are as hard as adamant.   God will " take away the heart of stone, and give a heart of flesh." Powerful lusts, though deeply fixed in our very nature, may be rooted up by the grace of Christ; even confirmed habits of sin may be destroyed.   Although the " Ethiopian cannot change his skin, or the leopard his spots," yet those who have long been in the habit of doing evil, may learn to do well.   God can raise up children to Abraham, out of the very stones; and the power which effects this is compared to that which effected the resurrection of the dead body of Christ from the grave.

The same grace is sufficient to preserve the soul in the midst of the strongest temptations.   He is able to keep his people unhurt in the most dangerous circumstances, even as the three confessors remained unsinged in the burning fiery furnace; or as Jonah was kept alive for three days and three nights in the belly of the fish. We daily witness the miracles of divine grace, as marvellous as if a stone were suspended in the air, or a spark kept alive in the ocean.   We are " kept by the power of God, through faith unto salvation."

Thus we see that sin is a most destructive evil—that every sinner is a self-destroyer,—and that there is help and salvation in Christ even for the self-destroying sinner.

IMPROVEMENT.—From the whole, let us learn, First,

to think rightly of sin. Here is the soul-ruining mistake of men. They are not told, or will not believe, that sin is of a destructive nature. Beware of slight thoughts of sin. Sin is no trifle. They are "fools only who make a mock at sin." "Be not deceived; God is not mocked; for whatsoever a man soweth that shall he also reap." "Let no man deceive you with vain words; for because of these things cometh the wrath of God upon the children of disobedience." Listen not, my friends —you especially who are young, listen not to your deluded companions, who would persuade you that there is no danger. Thus Satan deceived our first mother, and ruined the world. Beware, lest it ruin you. I entreat you to believe God, and disbelieve the enemy; yea, I may say, believe your ears; believe your eyes; believe your feelings; surely you may believe when you see around you so many horrid effects of sin, and hear, as it were, the groans of the damned, all uniting to say—Depend upon it, sin is a destructive evil. In the parable of the rich man and Lazarus, (Luke xvi. 19, &c.) the former, who, after a worldly life of self-indulgence, is represented as lifting up his eyes in torments, and in vain requesting the momentary relief of a drop of water to cool his tongue, requests that a messenger may be sent to his father's house, to testify to his surviving brethren, lest they also come into the same place of torment. What was the testimony he wished to be made to them? Was it not this—that sin, indulged, destroys the soul?—that sinners are, as has been shown, self-destroyers? But in vain did he request that such a message might be sent. It was needless. The same testimony had been made by Moses and the prophets, whom he and they refused to hear. The same testimony is now made to you. Oh, hear it, receive it, and act accordingly.

SERMON XIII.

SIN ODIOUS TO GOD.

Jeremiah xliv. 4.   Oh! do not this abominable thing that I hate.

THIS is part of a message sent from Jehovah, by his servant, the prophet Jeremiah, to a party of the Jews who retired to Egypt, when their brethren of Judah were led captive to Babylon.   God here reminds them of the reproofs he had given their nation, and of the punishments he had inflicted for its sins.   " I sent unto you (saith he) all my servants, the prophets, rising early and sending them;" and the substance of his messages by them was, " Oh! do not this abominable thing that I hate."

" The abominable thing" here referred to was, doubtless, their idolatry; they had " provoked him to anger, by burning incense to other gods," and by "pouring out drink-offerings to the queen of heaven." (verses 8, 17, &c.)   This sin was peculiarly hateful to God, for it robbed him of his glory as the only proper object of worship; it was a breach of his most positive commandments; and it was exceedingly criminal in *them*, for they were favoured above all nations with the knowledge of his nature and will; they were his appointed "witnesses," to testify to the world the unity of God; and this breach of their trust led them into undue connections with the heathen world, from which he had separated them, and induced them to commit many atrocious crimes insepa- rable from the worship of idols.   And their history shows how God resented this their conduct.   Neighbouring nations were let loose upon them for their punishment; and sometimes they were carried captive by their enemies; the ten tribes, who were the most idolatrous, were irre- coverably dispersed; and Judah herself was now captive in Babylon.   God, therefore, here exhorts them, by his

13 *

servant Jeremiah, to abstain from this provoking practice.
" Oh! do not this abominable thing that I hate."

But though this charge related originally to the idolatry
of Judah, it is properly applicable to sin in general, and
to every sin in particular :—and, oh, that every one of
us may consider the text as a message from God to himself, and particularly with relation to any " easily besetting
sin," of which he is conscious! And with this view, let
us notice three things contained in the words :

I. Sin is an abominable thing.

II. God hates it.

III. He requires us to avoid it. " Oh! do not this
abominable thing that I hate."

1. With regard to the real nature and evil of sin. We
must form our opinion of it, not from the world, but from
God. If we consult the world, in which " sin abounds,"
we shall find that " fools make a mock at it;" they treat
it as a trifle, which need not give them any uneasiness :
there are some who are properly " workers of iniquity ;"
it is their trade, yea, their food, their element, their delight ; they " cannot cease from sin :" and some go further
still ; they plead for it, they promote it in others, and
" glory in their shame."

But, whatever mistaken men, who are deceived and en-
slaved by the destroyer, may think of sin, we are sure
that our holy God, who cannot be deceived, and will not
deceive us, accounts it an abominable thing, and hates it
with a perfect hatred. And how can it be otherwise?
for it is exactly the reverse of all that he is, all that he
approves, and all that he requires. He gave us our being ;
he gave us all the powers of body and mind which we
possess. He gave us this earth on which we dwell ; and
he has filled it with his goodness. " He gives us rain
from heaven and fruitful seasons, and fills our hearts with
food and gladness." And all that he requires, and most
reasonably requires, by way of return, is that we love him
supremely, and that we love our neighbour as we wish he

should love us. And is not this most reasonable? Who can object to such a demand? But *does* man thus love his God, or his neighbour? Ah! no. The contrary is the fact. The hearts of men are by nature alienated from God, and their carnal minds are enmity against him. This will appear if you take a glance at the holy law, as it is summarily contained in the Ten Commandments.

The first commandment requires us to know and acknowledge Jehovah to be the only living and true God, and to worship and glorify him accordingly. But alas! how have vain men formed, in their corrupt imagination, " lords many and gods many !" they have multiplied deities, male and female, to the number of many thousands ! and thus they have given that glory to idols which is due to him alone !

The second commandment forbids the worship of God by images : but how fruitful have been the corrupt imaginations of men, in " changing the incorruptible glory of God into an image made like to corruptible man, and to birds, and to four-footed beasts, and creeping things !— offences so hateful to God, that he gave up these idolaters to the basest lusts of their own hearts. Rom. i.

How abominable to God is the profane, or even trifling, use of his most holy name !—a crime which though overlooked by men and magistrates, is such that the Majesty of heaven, so affronted, will not hold the offender guiltless, but will punish him as his iniquity deserves.

God, in mercy to mankind, has appointed one day in seven to be sacred to religion and to rest. But ungrateful man refuses this heavenly boon ; and while he robs God of his glory, in refusing obedience and worship, robs himself of the inestimable benefits he might enjoy.

God notices and hates the undutifulness and disobedience of children to their parents, while he gives a gracious promise to those who honour their father and mother.

How provoking to the Father of mercies is the crime

of murder! When the first murder was committed, "thy brother's blood (said God unto Cain) crieth to me from the earth;" it cried for vengeance; and the decision of justice is, "Whoso sheddeth man's blood, by man shall his blood be shed."

God has marked with peculiar infamy the sins of adultery and fornication; they are stamped with the name of "uncleanness," as being in a peculiar manner, contrary to that holiness which he requires of his creatures;—and let such offenders tremble when they read that "whoremongers and adulterers God will judge." Heb. xiii. 4. Yea, so infamous are these vices in his sight, that they must not even be named among saints. Eph. v. 4, 5.

Dishonesty, in all its forms, is offensive to the God of truth and equity. Not only open thieves, as housebreakers and highwaymen, are obnoxious to him, but all injustice between buyers and sellers; frauds committed in the price, weight, and measure of goods; all the arts of deception practised in trade; the dishonesty and negligence of servants; the contracting of debts without the prospect of payment;—in short, every transaction between man and man, contrary to that golden rule of action, "Whatsoever ye would that men should do to you, do ye even so to them."

Perjury is a sin of dreadful magnitude. Woe be to the man that feareth not an oath, or dare appeal to God for a lie! and all slander, malice, and wanton injury of the character of others, is an abomination in his view.

Covetousness he deems idolatry; for the (inordinate) love of money is the root of all evil; and as it is a secret sin, a sin of the heart, to which God alone may be witness,—it is an evil which, above all others, detects the true nature of sin. Paul says of himself, "he had not known lust (concupiscence, or sinful desire), unless the law had said, "Thou shalt not covet." Rom. vii. 7.

Thus have we seen, by a glance at the Ten Commandments, that sin is an abominable thing: the law proves it to be such, and his holy word calls it by names intended to express *his* abhorrence of it, and to excite *ours*;—it is "filthiness," 'poison," and an "abominable thing."

It is almost needless to prove, as we proposed, in the second place, that

God hates sin. "Oh! do not this abominable thing that I hate;" for, had he not hated it, he would not have prohibited it in his law, upon pain of death.

It must needs be hateful to him, for it has spoiled his work, especially the master-piece of his work upon earth, his creature Man, originally formed in his own holy image. Ah, how is that image defaced! how is that glorious creature degraded! Where now is his image? It is lost, it is gone; and the sinner, given up to the base lusts of his mind and his body, bears the horrible likeness of the devil and the brute combined : his wicked tempers resembling the former; his sordid appetites resembling the latter.

God's holy word is full of expressions of his just resentment :—" God is angry with the wicked every day." The wrath of God is revealed from heaven against all ungodliness and unrighteousness of men." "Thou hatest all workers of iniquity."

Hence also the dreadful threatenings which we find in his word: "The wages of sin is death:" "The wicked shall be turned into hell:"—"Say ye to the wicked, It shall be ill with him; for he shall eat of the fruit of his ways:"—"He that soweth to the flesh, shall of the flesh reap corruption."

And as the threatenings of God, in his word, denote his anger, so his proceedings in the world discover it too. What induced him to hurl from their high abodes in bliss, the myriads of angelic spirits, now enchained in darkness? Doubtless, it was their hateful sin against him. And what led him to expel from the garden of happiness the man whom he placed there to dress and to keep it? We know that it was his sinful disobedience. For the same cause, he who made the earth, " cursed it for man's sake;" doomed him to severe toil; and the woman to painful travail.   Hatred to sin " broke up all the fountains of the great deep, and opened all the windows (or floodgates) of heaven;" deluged the whole face of the earth, and drowned the human race.   It was God's just hatred to sin that led him to rain upon Sodom, and upon Gomorrah, brimstone and fire from the Lord out of heaven: to the same cause we owe all the dire diseases that invade the human frame, and render the earth one huge hospital: it is this that depopulates the globe thrice in a century, and fills the graves with unnumbered inhabitants; " for dust we are, and to dust must we return."   Nor is this all; there is a second death,—there is a dreadful hell for the reception and punishment of the wicked, where " their worm dieth not, and the fire is not quenched." To this horrible place He who hates sin will consign all finally impenitent and unbelieving sinners; saying, " Depart from me, ye cursed, into everlasting fire, prepared for the devil and his angels." And, now, is anything more necessary to prove that God hates sin?   One greater proof yet remains; it is this, the great, holy, and just Jehovah saw fit, in the exercise of his mercy towards men, to punish sin in the person of his innocent Son; " for what the law could not do, in that it was weak through the flesh," God hath been pleased to perform in a different manner: " he has sent his own Son, in the likeness of sinful flesh, and by a sacrifice for sin, condemned sin in the flesh," even in the human nature of Jesus Christ his only begotten Son; and this for his gracious purpose, " That the righteousness of God might be fulfilled *in* (or rather *for*) us, who walk not after the flesh, but after the Spirit." Rom. viii. 3, 4.

We have shown, 1, That sin is an abominable thing: and, 2, That God hates it: We now proceed to the last part of the subject, which is,

Thirdly, *God calls upon us to avoid sin.* "Oh! do not this abominable thing which I hate."

This, you see, was the substance of all his messages to Israel by the prophets :—"rising early, and sending them," alluding to the practice of men, who having business of great importance to transact, rise early to set about it, that no time may be lost; so God, earnest to prevent the destruction of men by their sins, sent his servants betimes to give them warning.

This is the language of the Ten Commandments; most of which, it is observable, are in the negative form; as do not kill, do not steal, do not bear false witness; and they are put in this form, because fallen man is disposed by nature to do that which is evil; he must, therefore, be warned against that evil to which he is prone. "Oh! do not this abominable thing that I hate." Let us remember and treasure up in our minds the word of God for this very purpose: thus David did. "Thy word (says he) have I hid in my heart, that I may not sin against thee :" and again, "How shall a young man cleanse his way?"—the answer is, "By taking heed thereunto, according to thy word :" and this proved successful; for he says again, "By the words of thy lips I have kept me from the paths of the Destroyer."

Observe also the heavenly discourse of our Saviour upon the mount? What divine morality is inculcated in that inimitable sermon! What a spiritual exposition does the King of Zion give of his holy law, to deter men from sin, and cause them to resemble their Father who is in heaven! In like manner the holy apostles, in their discourses and in the epistles, discourage every vice, and insist upon the sanctity of character which becomes christians; saying, "Let every one who nameth the name of Christ depart from iniquity."

The histories contained in the word of God have the same holy tendency. Do we read the histories of good men? "Let us be followers of them who, through faith and patience, inherit the promises." Do we peruse the histories of bad men, and of their sore punishment?— "these things are written for our warning,"—"these things happened unto them for examples; and they are written for our admonition upon whom the ends of the world are come." 1 Cor. x. 6—11.

The threatenings which we find in the word of God have the same benevolent intention. " Son of man (said God to the prophet Ezekiel), I have made thee a watchman unto the house of Israel, therefore hear the word at my mouth, and give them warning from me; when I say to the wicked, Thou shalt surely die, and thou givest him not warning, to save his life, the same wicked man shall die in his iniquity;—but his blood will I require at thy hand." Ezek. iii. 17. The language of all the threatenings is,—" Do not this abominable thing." "Turn ye, turn ye, for why will ye die, O house of Israel?"

And do not all the various blessings we receive from the hand of God come to us with the same message? Does he not do us good, giving us rain from heaven, and fruitful seasons, filling our hearts with food and gladness? Does not he visit the earth, and water it? clothe the pastures with flocks? cover the valleys with corn, and crown the year with his goodness? And doth not this goodness cry with a gentle yet powerful voice,—" Oh! do not this abominable thing that I hate?" And surely, if we will not hear that admonition, we shall hear him justly complain, " Hear, O heavens, and give ear, O earth; I have nourished and brought up children, and they have rebelled against me. The ox knoweth his owner, and the ass his master's crib; but Israel doth not know; my people doth not consider!"

And further, what is the language of affliction? What mean the numerous trials and troubles of life? Are they not all the fruits of sin? Do they not painfully convince us that sin is an evil and a bitter thing? And are they not intended for our profit, to introduce " the peaceable fruits of righteousness, and to make us partakers of his holiness?" Yes, every pain of body, and every pang of mind, says,—"Do not this abominable thing that I hate!"

In a word, such is the uniform language of the whole gospel of Christ. Is not this the doctrine of the Cross? Why did the innocent Son of God suffer, and bleed, and die? He did not sin, "neither was guile found in his mouth; yet it pleased the Lord to bruise him, and put him to grief; but he was wounded for our transgressions, he was bruised for our iniquities; the Lord laid upon him the iniquity of us all." In this way the all-wise God was pleased to exhibit to the whole world the just abhorrence of sin, by punishing it in the person of his Son, while he displays the riches of his grace in freely pardoning all who believe in him. Thus also he would furnish his people with the strongest possible motives to holiness, that they might hate the sin which murdered their Lord; and be constrained, by the force of love to him, to crucify the flesh with its affections and lusts, and to live unto him in holiness and righteousness of life all their days.

CONCLUSION.—And is sin such an abominable thing? —then "how abominable and filthy is man, that drinketh in iniquity like water?" (Job xv. 16.)—who longs for it as the parched traveller for the refreshing stream, and to whom it is as delightful as cold water to a thirsty soul; for there are those (are we of that number?) who commit iniquity with greediness; who take pleasure in unrighteousness; and who cannot cease from sin. Ah! how unlike are such men to God! and if only "the pure in heart shall see God," where shall these lovers and workers of iniquity appear? Marvel not, then, if to such we address the solemn words of Christ,—"Ye must be born again." "Verily, I say unto you, except a man be born again, he cannot see the kingdom of God," (John iii. 3, &c.)

This also shows how great and dangerous a mistake it

14

is, to think lightly of sin, or to esteem it a trifle ; or to do as the scripture says *"fools* do,"—"make a mock at sin." Ah! it is no trifle, unless the anger of an of-fended and Almighty God be a trifle, and unless everlast-ing punishment be a trifle. Oh, let us learn to think and speak of sin as *He* does who cannot be deceived, and will not be mocked.

It will follow, then, that if sin be so abominable in the sight of God, and if he so hate it, we also should hate it. So did Job, when his singular afflictions and in-structions had accomplished their designed purpose ; then did he exclaim—"I abhor myself, and repent in dust and ashes ;" and thus will it ever be found that penitent and pardoned sinners will "remember their own evil ways, and their doings that were not good, and lothe themselves in their own sight, for their iniquities, and for their abominations." Ezek. xxxvi. 31.

And this should lead us greatly to admire the love of God to such unlovely creatures as sinners are. His love must, indeed, be free, perfectly free, for there could be nothing in us to excite it ; there was enough to occasion his anger, and cause him to forsake us for ever; but while he held us in this low and lothesome state, "he passed by and beheld us, and said unto us, *Live !*" "for the time was a time of love!" (Ezek. xvi. 7.) Amazing love it was that said, "Come now, and let us reason to-gether, saith the Lord ; though your sins be as scarlet, they shall be as white as snow ; though they be red like crimson, they shall be as wool."

> Let all the world fall down, and know
> That none but God such love could show.

Here, too, let us admire the efficacy of the blood of Christ. Let us, with Peter, call it "precious blood," for precious indeed that blood must be which can perfectly cleanse from such horrid pollution, and make the believ-ing sinner, washed in that fountain, "whiter than snow."

Nor less admirable is the efficacious grace of the Holy
Spirit, through whose renewing power we become new
creatures; no longer "the slaves of sin," but rendered
"the servants of righteousness;" being "made free from
sin, we are become servants to God, having our fruit unto
holiness, and (expecting the blessed) end—"everlasting
life."

How strong, then, are the obligations under which we
are laid to "abhor that which is evil, and cleave unto
that which is good!" to "hate every false way, and the
garment spotted with the flesh;" to avoid even the appearance of evil, and to abound in every good work, continually walking as under the eye of God, and as hearing
him say to us,—"Oh! do not this abominable thing that
I hate."

A SELECTION

OF

PSALMS AND HYMNS

14*

A SELECTION

OF PSALMS AND HYMNS.

1

Providence. C. M.

GOD moves in a mysterious way,
His wonders to perform;
He plants his footsteps in the sea,
And rides upon the storm.

2 Deep in unfathomable mines
Of never failing skill,
He treasures up his bright designs,
And works his sovereign will.

3 Ye fearful saints, fresh courage take;
The clouds ye so much dread
Are big with mercy, and shall break
In blessings on your head.

4 Judge not the Lord by feeble sense,
But trust him for his grace;
Behind a frowning providence,
He hides a smiling face.

5 His purposes will ripen fast,
Unfolding every hour:
The bud may have a bitter taste,
But sweet will be the flower.

6 Blind unbelief is sure to err,
  And scan his work in vain;
God is his own interpreter,
  And he will make it plain.

———

2   *Come and Welcome.*   8s, 7s, & 4s.

COME, ye sinners, poor and wretched,
  Weak and wounded, sick and sore;
Jesus ready stands to save you,
  Full of pity, love and power :
    He is able,
  He is willing : doubt no more.

2 Ho ! ye needy, come and welcome,
  God's free bounty glorify;
True belief and true repentance,
  Every grace that brings us nigh,
    Without money,
  Come to Jesus Christ and buy.

3 Let not conscience make you linger,
  Nor of fitness fondly dream;
All the fitness he requireth,
  Is to feel your need of him;
    This he gives you;
  'Tis the Spirit's rising beam.

4 Come, ye weary, heavy laden,
  Lost and ruined by the fall:
If you tarry till you're better,
  You will never come at all.
    Not the righteous,
  Sinners Jesus came to call.

5 Agonizing in the garden,
  Lo ! your Maker prostrate lies;

On the bloody tree behold him;
Hear him cry, before he dies,
"It is finished!"
Sinner, will not this suffice?

6 Lo! the incarnate God ascended,
Pleads the merits of his blood;
Venture on him, venture wholly,
Let no other trust intrude;
None but Jesus
Can do helpless sinners good.

7 Saints and angels, joined in concert,
Sing the praises of the Lamb;
While the blissful seats of heaven
Sweetly echo with his name;
Hallelujah!
Sinners here may sing the same.

---

3   *The Holy Trinity.*   6s & 4s.

COME, thou Almighty King,
Help us thy name to sing,
Help us to praise.
Father all glorious,
O'er all victorious,
Come, and reign over us,
Ancient of days.

2 Jesus our Lord, arise,
Scatter our enemies,
And make them fall.
Let thine Almighty aid
Our sure defence be made;
Our souls on thee be staid;
Lord, hear our call.

3 Come, thou incarnate Word,
Gird on thy mighty sword,
  Our prayer attend.
    Come, and thy people bless,
    And give thy word success;
    Spirit of holiness,
On us descend.

4 Come, Holy Comforter,
Thy sacred witness bear,
  In this glad hour.
    Thou, who almighty art,
    Now rule in every heart,
    And ne'er from us depart,
Spirit of power.

5 To the great One in Three,
The highest praises be,
  Hence evermore.
    His sovereign majesty,
    May we in glory see,
    And to eternity,
Love and adore.

———

4   *The Lord will provide.*   10s & 11s.

THOUGH troubles assail, and dangers affright;
    Though friends should all fail, and foes all unite;
Yet one thing secures us, whatever betide;
The scripture assures us, the Lord will provide.

2 The birds, without barn or store-house, are fed;
From them let us learn to trust for our bread:
His saints what is fitting shall ne'er be denied;
So long as 'tis written, the Lord will provide.

3 We may, like the ships, by tempests be tossed
On perilous deeps, but cannot be lost;
Though Satan enrages the wind and the tide,
The promise engages, the Lord will provide.

4 His call we obey, like Abram of old,
Not knowing our way, but faith makes us bold;
For though we are strangers, we have a good guide,
And trust in all dangers, the Lord will provide.

5 When Satan appears to stop up our path,
And fills us with fears, we triumph by faith :
He cannot take from us, though oft he has tried,
This heart-cheering promise, the Lord will provide.

6 He tells us we're weak, our hope is in vain :
The good, that we seek, we ne'er shall obtain;
But when such suggestions our spirits have plied,
This answers all questions, the Lord will provide.

7 No strength of our own, or goodness we claim,
Yet since we have known the Saviour's great name,
In this our strong tower for safety we hide :
The Lord is our power, the Lord will provide.

8 When life sinks apace, and death is in view,
This word of his grace shall comfort us through :
No fearing or doubting, with Christ on our side,
We hope to die shouting, the Lord will provide.

———

5   *Sovereign Grace.*   S. M.

GRACE ! 'tis a charming sound,
     Harmonious to mine ear ·
Heaven with the echo shall resound,
     And all the earth shall hear.

2 Grace first contrived the way
    To save rebellious man,
And all the steps *that* grace display,
    Which.drew the wondrous plan.

3 Grace first inscribed my name
    In God's eternal book ;
'Twas grace that gave me to the Lamb,
    Who all my sorrows took.

4 Grace led my roving feet
    To tread the heavenly road ;
And new supplies each hour I meet,
    While pressing on to God.

5 Grace taught my soul to pray,
    And made my eyes o'erflow :
'Twas grace that kept me to this day,
    And will not let me go.

6 Grace all the work shall crown,
    Through everlasting days ;
It lays in heaven the topmost stone,
    And well deserves the praise.

————

6   *The Rock of Ages.*   7s.

ROCK of ages, cleft for me,
    Let me hide myself in thee ·
Let the water and the blood,
From thy wounded side which flowed,
Be of sin the double cure ;
Cleanse me from its guilt and power.

2 Not the labour of my hands
    Can fulfil the law's demands ;
Could my zeal no respite know,
Could my tears for ever flow,

All for sin could not atone,
Thou must save, and thou alone.

3 Nothing in my hand I bring,
Simply to thy cross I cling;
Naked, come to thee for dress,
Helpless, look to thee for grace,
Vile, I to the fountain fly,—
Wash me, Saviour, or I die.

4 While I draw this fleeting breath,
When my heart-strings break in death,
When I soar to worlds unknown,
See thee on thy judgment-throne,—
Rock of ages, cleft for me,
Let me hide myself in thee.

---

7   *The Death of Christ.*   S. M.

LIKE sheep we went astray,
    And broke the fold of God;
Each wandering in a different way,
    But all the downward road.

2 How dreadful was the hour,
    When God our wanderings laid,
And did at once his vengeance pour
    Upon the Shepherd's head!

3 How glorious was the grace
    When Christ sustained the stroke!
His life and blood the Shepherd pays,
    A ransom for the flock.

4 His honour and his breath
    Were taken both away;
Joined with the wicked in his death,
    And made as vile as they.

15

5 But God shall raise his head
   O'er all the sons of men,
And make him see a numerous seed,
   To recompense his pain.

6 " I'll give him," saith the Lord,
   " A portion with the strong;
He shall possess a large reward,
   And hold his honours long."

----

8   *Doubts and Fears.*

'TIS a point I long to know,
   Oft it causes anxious thought;
Do I love the Lord, or no?
   Am I his, or am I not?

2 If I love, why am I thus?
   Why this dull and lifeless frame?
Hardly, sure, can they be worse,
   Who have never heard his name.

3 Could my heart so hard remain,
   Prayer a task and burden prove,
Every trifle give me pain,
   If I knew a Saviour's love?

4 When I turn my eyes within,
   All is dark, and vain, and wild;
Filled with unbelief and sin,
   Can I deem myself a child?

5 If I pray, or hear, or read,
   Sin is mixed with all I do;
You who love the Lord indeed,
   Tell me—is it thus with you?

6 Yet I mourn my stubborn will,
   Find my sin a grief and thrall;

Should I grieve for what I feel,
　If I did not love at all?

7 Could I joy his saints to meet,
　Choose the ways I once abhorred,
Find at times the promise sweet,
　If I did not love the Lord?

8 Lord, decide the doubtful case;
　Thou who art thy people's Sun,
Shine upon thy work of grace,
　If it be indeed begun.

9 Let me love thee more and more,
　If I love at all, I pray;
If I have not loved before,
　Help me to begin to-day.

———

9　　　*Not ashamed of Christ.*　C. M.

I'M not ashamed to own my Lord,
　Nor to defend his cause,
Maintain the honour of his word,
　The glory of his cross.

2 Jesus, my God, I know his name,
　His name is all my trust;
Nor will he put my soul to shame,
　Nor let my hope be lost.

3 Firm as his throne his promise stands,
　And he can well secure
What I've committed to his hands,
　Till the decisive hour.

4 Then will he own my worthless name,
　Before his Father's face,
And in the new Jerusalem,
　Appoint my soul a place.

10   *Not ashamed of Christ.* L. M.

JESUS, and shall it ever be,
   A mortal man ashamed of thee?
Ashamed of thee, whom angels praise,
Whose glories shine through endless days!

2 Ashamed of Jesus! sooner far
Let evening blush to own a star;
He sheds the beams of light divine
O'er this benighted soul of mine.

3 Ashamed of Jesus! just as soon
Let midnight be ashamed of noon;
'Tis midnight with my soul, till he,
Bright morning Star, bid darkness flee.

4 Ashamed of Jesus! that dear Friend
On whom my hopes of heaven depend!
No, when I blush, be this my shame,
That I no more revere his name.

5 Ashamed of Jesus! Yes, I may,
When I've no guilt to wash away,
No tear to wipe, no good to crave,
No fears to quell, no soul to save.

6 Till then—nor is my boasting vain—
Till then, I boast a Saviour slain
And oh! may this my glory be,
That Christ is not ashamed of me.

---

11   *Refuge in Christ.* 7s.

JESUS, lover of my soul,
   Let me to thy bosom fly,
While the raging billows roll,
   While the tempest still is high.

Hide me, O my Saviour, hide,
 Till the storm of life is past;
Safe into the haven guide;
 Oh! receive my soul at last.

2 Other refuge have I none,
 Hangs my helpless soul on thee;
Leave, ah! leave me not alone,
 Still support and comfort me;
All my trust on thee is staid,
 All my help from thee I bring;
Cover my defenceless head
 With the shadow of thy wing.

3 Thou, O Christ, art all I want;
 All in all in thee I find;
Raise the fallen, cheer the faint,
 Heal the sick, and lead the blind.
Just and holy is thy name
 I am all unrighteousness ·
Vile and full of sin I am,
 Thou art full of truth and grace.

4 Plenteous grace with thee is found,
 Grace to pardon all my sin;
Let the healing streams abound,
 Make and keep me pure within.
Thou of life the fountain art,
 Freely let me take of thee:
Spring thou up within my heart,
 Rise to all eternity.

---

12   *Joy in Christ.* 8s & 7s.

COME, thou Fount of every blessing,
 Tune my heart to sing thy grace;
Streams of mercy never ceasing
 Call for songs of loudest praise

15 *

Teach me some melodious sonnet,
    Sung by flaming tongues above;
Praise the mount—Oh! fix me on it,
    Mount of God's unchanging love.

2 Here I raise my Ebenezer,
    Hither by thy help I'm come;
And I hope, by thy good pleasure,
    Safely to arrive at home.
Jesus sought me when a stranger,
    Wandering from the fold of God;
He, to rescue me from danger,
    Interposed with precious blood.

3 Oh! to grace how great a debtor
    Daily I'm constrained to be!
Let that grace, Lord, like a fetter,
    Bind my wandering heart to thee.
Prone to wander, Lord, I feel it;
    Prone to leave the God I love;
Here's my heart, Lord, take and seal it,
    Seal it from thy courts above.

---

13   *The Lord's Day.* S. M.

WELCOME, sweet day of rest,
    That saw the Lord arise;
Welcome to this reviving breast,
    And these rejoicing eyes.

2 The King himself comes near,
    And feasts his saints to-day;
Here we may sit, and see him here,
    And love and praise and pray.

3 One day amidst the place
    Where my dear God hath been,
Is sweeter than ten thousand days
    Of pleasurable sin.

4 My willing soul would stay
　　In such a frame as this,
And sit and sing herself away
　　To everlasting bliss.

14　　　　*Christ our Shepherd.*　S. M.

THE Lord my Shepherd is,
　　I shall be well supplied;
Since he is mine, and I am his,
　　What can I want beside?

2 He leads me to the place
　　Where heavenly pasture grows;
Where living waters gently pass,
　　And full salvation flows.

3 If e'er I go astray,
　　He doth my soul reclaim,
And guides me in his own right way,
　　For his most holy name.

4 While he affords his aid,
　　I cannot yield to fear;
Tho' I should walk thro' death's dark shade,
　　My Shepherd's with me there.

5 Amid surrounding foes
　　Thou dost my table spread,
My cup with blessings overflows,
　　And joy exalts my head.

6 The bounties of thy love
　　Shall crown my following days;
Nor from thy house will I remove,
　　Nor cease to speak thy praise.

15   *The Penitent's Psalm.*   L. M.

SHOW pity, Lord; O Lord, forgive,
    Let a repenting rebel live;
Are not thy mercies large and free?
May not a sinner trust in thee?

2 My crimes are great, but don't surpass
The power and glory of thy grace;
Great God, thy nature hath no bound,
So let thy pardoning love be found.

3 Oh! wash my soul from every sin,
And make my guilty conscience clean;
Here on my heart the burden lies,
And past offences pain my eyes.

4 My lips with shame my sins confess,
Against thy law, against thy grace;
Lord, should thy judgments grow severe,
I am condemned, but thou art clear.

5 Should sudden vengeance seize my breath,
I must pronounce thee just in death;
And if my soul were sent to hell,
Thy righteous law approves it well.

6 Yet save a trembling sinner, Lord,
Whose hope, still hovering round thy word,
Would light on some sweet promise there,
Some sure support against despair.

———

16   *The Lord's Day.*   L. M.

SWEET is the work, my God, my King,
    To praise thy name, give thanks, and sing,
To show thy love by morning light,
And talk of all thy truth at night.

2 Sweet is the day of sacred rest;
No mortal care shall seize my breast;

Oh! may my heart in tune be found
Like David's harp of solemn sound;

3 My heart shall triumph in my Lord,
And bless his works, and bless his word;
Thy works of grace, how bright they shine!
How deep thy counsels! how divine!

4 Fools never raise their thoughts so high;
Like brutes they live, like brutes they die;
Like grass they flourish, till thy breath
Blast them in everlasting death.

5 But I shall share a glorious part,
When grace hath well refined my heart,
And fresh supplies of joy are shed,
Like holy oil to cheer my head.

6 Sin, my worst enemy before,
Shall vex my eyes and ears no more;
My inward foes shall all be slain,
Nor Satan break my peace again.

7 Then shall I see, and hear, and know
All I desired or wished below;
And every power find sweet employ
In that eternal world of joy.

———

17   *Psalm before Hearing the Word.*   S. M.

COME, sound his praise abroad,
  And hymns of glory sing;
Jehovah is the sovereign God,
  The universal King.

2 He formed the deeps unknown;
  He gave the seas their bound;
The watery worlds are all his own,
  And all the solid ground.

3 Come, worship at his throne,
    Come, bow before the Lord ;
We are his works, and not our own :
    He formed us by his word.

4 To-day attend his voice
    Nor dare provoke his rod ;
Come, like the people of his choice,
    And own your gracious God.

5 But if your ears refuse
    The language of his grace,
And hearts grow hard, like stubborn Jews,
    That unbelieving race ·

6 The Lord, in vengeance drest,
    Will lift his hand and swear,
" You that despise my promised rest,
    Shall have no portion there."

---

18   *Praise.*   S. M.

O BLESS the Lord, my soul,
    Let all within me join,
And aid my tongue to bless his name,
    Whose favours are divine.

2 O bless the Lord, my soul,
    Nor let his mercies lie
Forgotten in unthankfulness,
    And without praises die.

3 'Tis he forgives thy sins,
    'Tis he relieves thy pain,
'Tis he that heals thy sicknesses,
    And makes thee young again.

4 He crowns thy life with love,
　　When ransomed from the grave;
　He that redeemed my soul from hell
　　˙Hath sovereign power to save.

5 He fills the poor with good;
　　He gives the sufferers rest;
　The Lord hath judgments for the proud,
　　And justice for th' oppressed.

6 His wondrous works and ways
　　He made by Moses known;
　But sent the world his truth and grace
　　By his beloved Son.

————

19　　　　　*God never forsakes.*　11s.

HOW firm a foundation, ye saints of the Lord,
　　Is laid for your faith in his excellent word!
What more can he say than to you he hath said,
You who unto Jesus for refuge have fled?

2 In every condition—in sickness, in health,
In poverty's vale, or abounding in wealth,
At home and abroad, on the land, on the sea,
" As thy days may demand, shall thy strength ever be.

3 " Fear not, I am with thee, O! be not dismayed,
I, I am thy God, and will still give thee aid;
I'll strengthen thee, help thee, and cause thee to stand,
Upheld by my righteous, omnipotent hand.

4 " When through the deep waters I call thee to go,
The rivers of woe shall not thee overflow;
For I will be with thee, thy troubles to bless;
And sanctify to thee, thy deepest distress.

5 " When through fiery trials thy pathway shall lie,
My grace all-sufficient shall be thy supply ;
The flame shall not hurt thee ; I only design
Thy dross to consume, and thy gold to refine.

6 " E'en down to old age, all my people shall prove
My sovereign, eternal, unchangeable love ;
And when hoary hairs shall their temples adorn,
Like lambs they shall still in my bosom be borne.

7 "The soul that on Jesus hath leaned for repose,
I will not, I will not, desert to his foes ;
That soul, though all hell should endeavour to shake,
I'll never, no never, no never forsake '

---

20   *Repentance at the Cross.*   C. M.

ALAS ! and did my Saviour bleed,
    And did my Sovereign die ?
Would he devote that sacred head
    For such a worm as I ?

2 Thy body slain, dear Jesus, thine,
    And bathed in its own blood ;
While all exposed to wrath divine,
    The glorious sufferer stood !

3 Was it for crimes that I had done,
    He groaned upon the tree ?
Amazing pity ! grace unknown '
    And love beyond degree !

4 Well might the sun in darkness hide,
    And shut his glories in,
When God, the mighty Maker, died,
    For man, the creature's sin.

5 Thus might I hide my blushing face,
    While his dear cross appears,
Dissolve my heart in thankfulness,
    And melt my eyes to tears.

6 But drops of grief can ne'er repay
    The debt of love I owe :
Here, Lord, I give myself away ;
    'Tis all that I can do.

---

21   *Evening.*   S. M.

THE day is past and gone,
    The evening shades appear ;
Oh ! may we all remember well,
    The night of death draws near.

2 We lay our garments by,
    Upon our beds to rest ;
So death will soon disrobe us all
    Of what is here possessed.

3 Lord, keep us safe this night,
    Secure from all our fears ;
May angels guard us, while we sleep,
    Till morning light appears.

4 And when we early rise,
    And view the unwearied sun,
May we set out to win the prize,
    And after glory run.

5 And when our days are past,
    And we from time remove,
Oh ! may we in thy bosom rest,
    The bosom of thy love.

16

22   *Missionary Hymn.*   7s & 6s.

FROM Greenland's icy mountains,
      From India's coral strand;
Where Afric's sunny fountains
      Roll down their golden sand;
From many an ancient river,
      From many a palmy plain,
They call us to deliver
      Their land from error's chain.

2 What, though the spicy breezes
      Blow soft o'er Ceylon's isle,
Though every prospect pleases,
      And only man is vile;
In vain with lavish kindness,
      The gifts of God are strown;
The heathen, in his blindness,
      Bows down to wood and stone.

3 Shall we, whose souls are lighted
      With wisdom from on high,—
Shall we, to men benighted,
      The lamp of life deny?
Salvation! O salvation!
      The joyful sound proclaim,
Till earth's remotest nation
      Has learned Messiah's name.

4 Waft, waft, ye winds, his story,
      And you, ye waters, roll,
Till, like a sea of glory,
      It spreads from pole to pole;
Till o'er our ransomed nature,
      The Lamb for sinners slain,
Redeemer, King, Creator,
      In bliss returns to reign.

23 *On Watch.* L. M.

MY God, permit me not to be
    A stranger to myself and thee;
Amidst a thousand thoughts I rove,
Forgetful of my highest love.

2 Why should my passions mix with earth,
And thus debase my heavenly birth?
Why should I cleave to things below,
And let my God, my Saviour, go?

3 Call me away from flesh and sense;
One sovereign word can draw me thence;
I would obey the voice divine,
And all inferior joys resign.

4 Be earth, with all her scenes, withdrawn;
Let noise and vanity be gone;
In secret silènce of the mind,
My heaven, and there my God, I find.

———

24 *Consolation in Sickness.* C. M.

WHEN languor and disease invade
    This trembling house of clay,
'Tis sweet to look beyond my pains,
And long to fly away.

2 Sweet to look inward, and attend
The whispers of his love;
Sweet to look upward, to the place
Where Jesus pleads above.

3 Sweet to look back, and see my name
In life's fair book set down;
Sweet to look forward, and behold
Eternal joys my own.

4 Sweet to reflect how grace divine
    My sins on Jesus laid;
Sweet to remember that his blood
    My debt of suffering paid.

5 Sweet in his righteousness to stand,
    Which saves from second death;
Sweet to experience, day by day,
    His Spirit's quickening breath.

6 Sweet on his faithfulness to rest,
    Whose love can never end;
Sweet on his covenant of grace,
    For all things to depend.

7 Sweet in the confidence of faith,
    To trust his firm decrees;
Sweet to lie passive in his hands,
    And know no will but his.

8 If such the sweetness of the streams,
    What must the fountain be,
Where saints and angels draw their bliss
    Immediately from thee!

25   *Triumph over Death.*   C. M.

OH! for an overcoming faith
    To cheer my dying hours,
To triumph o'er the monster, Death,
    And all his frightful powers!

2 Joyful, with all the strength I have,
    My quivering lips should sing:
"Where is thy boasted victory, grave,
    And where the monster's sting?"

3 If sin be pardoned, I'm secure;
    Death has no sting beside;

The law gives sin its damning power;
But Christ, my ransom, died.

4 Now to the God of victory
   Immortal thanks be paid,
Who makes us conquerors while we die,
   Through Christ our living head.

26   *Heaven.*   C. M.

JERUSALEM, my happy home,
   Name ever dear to me!
When shall my labours have an end,
   In joy, and peace, and thee?

2 When shall these eyes thy heaven-built walls
   And pearly gates behold?
Thy bulwarks, with salvation strong,
   And streets of shining gold?

3 Oh! when, thou city of my God,
   Shall I thy courts ascend,
Where congregations ne'er break up,
   And Sabbaths have no end?

4 There happier bowers than Eden's bloom,
   Nor sin nor sorrow know:
Blest seats, through rude and stormy scenes,
   I onward press to you

5 Why should I shrink at pain and woe,
   Or feel at death, dismay?
I've Canaan's goodly land in view,
   And realms of endless day.

6 Apostles, martyrs, prophets there
   Around my Saviour stand;
And soon my friends in Christ below,
   Will join the glorious band.

16 *

7 Jerusalem, my happy home,
My soul still pants for thee;
Then shall my labours have an end,
When I thy joys shall see.

---

27 *Resurrection.* L. M.

LORD, I am thine; but thou wilt prove
My faith, my patience, and my love:
When men of spite against me join,
They are the sword, the hand is thine.

2 Their hope and portion lie below;
'Tis all the happiness they know;
'Tis all they seek, they take their shares,
And leave the rest among their heirs.

3 What sinners value, I resign;
Lord, 'tis enough that thou art mine:
I shall behold thy blissful face,
And stand complete in righteousness.

4 This life's a dream, an empty show;
But the bright world to which I go
Hath joys substantial and sincere;
When shall I wake and find me there?

5 O glorious hour! O blest abode!
I shall be near, and like my God;
And flesh and sin no more control
The sacred pleasures of the soul.

6 My flesh shall slumber in the ground,
Till the last trumpet's joyful sound;
Then burst the chains with sweet surprise,
And in my Saviour's image rise.

28   *Judgment.*   L. C. M.

L O ! on a narrow neck of land,
    'Twixt two unbounded seas I stand,
    Yet how insensible !
A point of time, a moment's space,
Removes me to yon heavenly place,
    Or shuts me up in hell.

2 O God, my inmost soul convert,
    And deeply on my thoughtless heart,
        Eternal things impress;
    Give me to feel their solemn weight,
    And save me ere it be too late;
        Wake me to righteousness.

3 Before me place in bright array,
    The pomp of that tremendous day,
        When thou with clouds shalt come
    To judge the nations at thy bar:
    And tell me, Lord, shall I be there,
        To meet a joyful doom?

4 Be this my one great business here,
    With holy trembling, holy fear,
        To make my calling sure;
    Thine utmost counsel to fulfil,
    And suffer all thy righteous will,
        And to the end endure.

5 Then, Saviour, then my soul receive,
    Transported from this vale, to live
        And reign with thee above;
    Where faith is sweetly lost in sight,
    And hope, in full, supreme delight,
        And everlasting love.

29   *Assurance of Heaven.*   C. M.

WHEN I can read my title clear,
    To mansions in the skies,
I bid farewell to every fear,
    And wipe my weeping eyes.

2 Should earth against my soul engage,
    And hellish darts be hurled;
Then I can smile at Satan's rage
    And face a frowning world.

3 Let cares like a wild deluge come,
    And storms of sorrow fall;
May I but safely reach my home,
    My God, my heaven, my all.

4 There shall I bathe my weary soul
    In seas of heavenly rest,
And not a wave of trouble roll
    Across my peaceful breast.

---

30   *After a Storm.*   L. M.

WOULD you behold the works of God,
    His wonders in the world abroad?
With the bold mariners survey
The unknown regions of the sea.

2 They leave their native shores behind,
And seize the favour of the wind;
Till God command, and tempests rise,
That heave the ocean to the skies.

3 Now to the heavens they mount amain,
Now sink to dreadful deeps again;
What strange affrights young sailors feel,
And like a staggering drunkard reel!

4 When land is far and death is nigh,
Lost to all hope, to God they cry;
His mercy hears their loud address,
And sends salvation in distress.

5 He bids the winds their wrath assuage,
And stormy tempests cease to rage;
The gladsome crew their fears give o'er,
And hail with joy their native shore.

6 Oh! may the sons of men record
The wondrous goodness of the Lord!
Let them their private offerings bring,
And in the church his glory sing.

---

31   *Seaman's Prayer in Danger.*   12s.

WHEN through the torn sail the wild tempest is
        streaming,
When o'er the dark wave the red lightning is gleam-
ing,
Nor hope lends a ray, the poor seaman to cherish,
We fly to our Maker; "Save, Lord, or we perish."

2 O Jesus, once rocked on the breast of the billow,
Aroused by the shriek of despair from thy pillow,
Now seated in glory, the mariner cherish,
Who cries in his anguish, "Save, Lord, or we perish."

3 And oh! when the whirlwind of passion is raging,
When sin in our hearts his wild warfare is waging,
Then send down thy grace, thy redeemed to cherish,
Rebuke the destroyer; "Save, Lord, or we perish."

32   *The Traveller's Hymn.*   C. M.

HOW are thy servants blest, O Lord,
How sure is their defence !
Eternal wisdom is their guide,
Their help, Omnipotence.

2 In foreign realms and lands remote,
Supported by thy care,
Through burning climes they pass unhurt,
And breathe in tainted air.

3 When by the dreadful tempest borne
High on the broken wave,
They know thou art not slow to hear,
Nor impotent to save.

4 The storm is laid, the winds retire,
Obedient to thy will;
The sea, that roars at thy command,
At thy command is still.

5 In midst of dangers, fears, and deaths,
Thy goodness we'll adore;
We'll praise thee for thy mercies past,
And humbly hope for more.

6 Our life, while thou preserv'st that life,
Thy sacrifice shall be:
And death, when death shall be our lot,
Shall join our souls to thee.

---

33   *The Voyage.*   H. M.

JESUS, at thy command
I launch into the deep,
And leave my native land,
Where sin lulls all asleep:
For thee I would the world resign,
And sail to heaven with thee and thine.

2 Thou art my pilot wise;
   My compass is thy word:
My soul each storm defies,
   While I have such a Lord!
I trust thy faithfulness and power
To save me in the trying hour

3 Though rocks and quicksands deep
   Through all my passage lie;
Yet Christ will safely keep
   And guide me with his eye:
My anchor, Hope, shall firm abide,
And I each boisterous storm outride.

4 By faith I see the land—
   The port of endless rest:
My soul, thy sails expand,
   And fly to Jesus' breast!
Oh! may I reach the heavenly shore,
Where winds and waves distress no more.

5 Whene'er becalmed I lie,
   And storms forbear to toss;
Be thou, dear Lord, still nigh,
   Lest I should suffer loss:
For more the treacherous calm I dread,
Than tempest bursting o'er my head.

6 Come, Holy Ghost, and blow
   A prosperous gale of grace;
Waft me from all below
   To heaven—my destined place!
Then, in full sail, my port I'll find,
And leave the world and sin behind.

34   *The desired Port.*   L. M.

THE christian navigates a sea
    Where various forms of death appear;
Nor skill, alas! nor power has he,
    Aright his dangerous course to steer.

2 Sometimes there lies a treacherous rock
    Beneath the surface of the wave;
He strikes, but yet survives the shock,
    For Jesus is at hand to save.

3 But hark! the midnight tempest roars!
    He seems forsaken and alone;
But Jesus whom he then implores,
    Unseen preserves and leads him on.

4 On the smooth surface of the deep,
    Without a fear he sometimes lies:
The danger then is lest he sleep,
    And ruin seize him by surprise.

5 His destined land he sometimes sees,
    And thinks his toils will soon be o'er;
Expects some favourable breeze
    Will waft him quickly to the shore.

6 But sudden clouds obstruct his view,
    And he enjoys the sight no more;
Nor does he now believe it true,
    That he had even seen the shore.

7 Though fear his heart should overwhelm,
    He'll reach the port for which he's bound;
For Jesus holds and guides the helm,
    And safety is where he is found.

35   *Christ in the storm.*   C. M

ETERNAL God, thy works of might
 Our awe and wonder raise;
Thy deeds of glory far surpass
 Our loftiest notes of praise.

2 Thine awful thunder fills the air,
 Resounding through the sky,
While vivid lightnings, 'mid the gloom,
 Proclaim Jehovah nigh.

3 He comes; all nature prostrate lies,
 And trembles at his nod;
Earthquakes and dreadful storms announce
 The presence of our God.

4 The howling winds, the beating rain,
 The sea's tumultuous roar,
These, in tremendous concert joined,
 Exalt thy boundless power.

5 Great God, we trust the matchless strength
 Of thine almighty arm,
Which, 'mid the wreck of thousand worlds,
 Could shelter us from harm.

—————

36   *All's well.*   8s & 7s.

TOSSED upon life's raging billow,
 Sweet it is, O Lord, to know
Thou didst press a sailor's pillow,
 And canst feel a sailor's woe.
Never slumbering, never sleeping,
 Though the night be dark and drear,
Thou the faithful watch art keeping,
 " All, all's well," thy constant cheer.

17

2 And though loud the wind is howling,
    Fierce though flash the lightnings red,
Darkly though the storm cloud's scowling
    O'er the sailor's anxious head,
Thou canst calm the raging ocean,
    All its noise and tumult still,
Hush the tempest's wild commotion,
    At the bidding of thy will.

3 Thus my heart the hope will cherish,
    While to thee I lift mine eye,
I shall ne'er be left to perish ,
    Thou wilt hear the sailor's cry ;
And though mast and sail be riven,
    Life's short cruise will soon be o'er;
On the peaceful shore of heaven,
    Wind and waves shall vex no more.

---

37   *Prayer for Seamen.*   L. M.

GRANT the abundance of the sea,
    May be converted, Lord, to thee,
And every sailor on the shore
Return to God, to roam no more.

2 The nations, then, with joy shall hail
The Bethel flag in every sail ;
And every ship that ploughs the sea
A gospel messenger shall be.

3 Hasten, O Lord, that glorious day
When seamen shall thy word obey,
And safe from port to port be driven
To point a ruined world to heaven.

38 *The cleansing Fountain.* C. M.

THERE is a fountain filled with blood,
  Drawn from Immanuel's veins ;
And sinners, plunged beneath that flood,
  Lose all their guilty stains.

2 The dying thief rejoiced to see
  That fountain in his day ;
And there have I, as vile as he,
  Washed all my sins away.

3 Dear dying Lamb, thy precious blood
  Shall never lose its power,
Till all the ransomed church of God
  Be saved, to sin no more.

4 E'er since, by faith, I saw the stream
  Thy flowing wounds supply,
Redeeming love has been my theme,
  And shall be, till I die.

5 Then in a nobler, sweeter song,
  I'll sing thy power to save,
When this poor lisping, stammering tongue
  Lies silent in the grave.

---

39 *The Sinner's Friend.* 8s & 7s.

ONE there is above all others,
  Well deserves the name of Friend ;
His is love beyond a brother's,
  Costly, free, and knows no end.
They who once his kindness prove
Find it everlasting love.

2 Which of all our friends, to save us,
    Could or would have shed his blood?
But this Saviour died to have us
    Reconciled in him to God.
This was boundless love indeed;
Jesus is a Friend in need.

3 When he lived on earth abased,
    Friend of sinners was his name;
Now above all glory raised,
    He rejoices in the same.
Still he calls them brethren, friends,
And to all their wants attends.

4 Oh for grace our hearts to soften!
    Teach us, Lord, at length to love;
We, alas! forgot too often
    What a friend we have above;
But when home our souls are brought,
We will love thee as we ought.

---

40   *The True Christian.*   L. M.

WHO shall ascend thy heavenly place,
    Great God, and dwell before thy face?
The man who minds religion now,
And humbly walks with God below;

2 Whose hands are pure, whose heart is clean;
Whose lips still speak the thing they mean,
No slanders dwell upon his tongue;
He hates to do his neighbour wrong.

3 He loves his enemies, and prays
For those who curse him to his face;
And does to all men still the same
That he would hope or wish from them.

4 Yet when his holiest works are done,
His soul depends on grace alone :
This is the man thy face shall see,
And dwell for ever, Lord, with thee.

---

41   *The Mariner's Psalm.*   C. M.

THY works of glory, mighty Lord,
   Who rul'st the boisterous sea,
The sons of courage shall record,
   Who tempt the dangerous way.

2 At thy command the winds arise,
   And swell the towering waves !
The men, astonished, mount the skies,
   And sink in gaping graves.

3 Again they climb the watery hills,
   And plunge in deeps again ;
Each like a tottering drunkard reels,
   And finds his courage vain.

4 Frighted to hear the tempest roar,
   They pant with fluttering breath ;
And, hopeless of the distant shore,
   Expect immediate death.

5 Then to the Lord they raise their cries,
   He hears the loud request,
And orders silence through the skies,
   And lays the floods to rest.

6 Sailors rejoice to lose their fears,
   And see the storm allayed :
Now to their eyes the port appears ;
   There let their vows be paid.

7 'Tis God that brings them safe to land;
     Let stupid mortals know,
That waves are under his command,
     And all the winds that blow.

8 Oh that the sons of men would praise
     The goodness of the Lord!
And those that see thy wondrous ways,
     Thy wondrous love record.

---

42   *Prospect of Death.*   8s & 7s.

GENTLY, Lord, O gently lead us,
     Through this lonely vale of tears;
Through the changes thou'st decreed us,
     Till our last great change appears.
When temptation's darts assail us,
     When in devious paths we stray,
Let thy goodness never fail us,
     Lead us in thy perfect way.

2 In the hour of pain and anguish,
     In the hour when death draws near,
Suffer not our hearts to languish,
     Suffer not our souls to fear.
And when mortal life is ended,
     Bid us in thine arms to rest,
Till by angel bands attended,
     We awake among the blest.

DOXOLOGIES.

C. M.

LET God the Father, and the Son,
     And Spirit be adored,
Where there are works to make him known,
     Or saints to love the Lord.

C. M.

TO Father, Son, and Holy Ghost,
   The God whom we adore,
Be glory as it was, is now,
   And shall be evermore.

L. M.

PRAISE God from whom all blessings flow;
   Praise him, all creatures here below;
Praise him above, ye heavenly host;
Praise Father, Son, and Holy Ghost.

L. M.

TO God the Father, God the Son,
   And God the Spirit, Three in One,
Be honour, praise, and glory given,
By all on earth, and all in heaven.

S. M.

YE angels round the throne,
   And saints that dwell below,
Worship the Father, love the Son,
   And bless the Spirit too.

S. M.

GIVE to the Father praise,
   Give glory to the Son,
And to the Spirit of his grace
   Be equal honour done.

H. M.

TO God the Father's throne,
   Perpetual honours raise:
Glory to God the Son;
   To God the Spirit praise:
With all our powers, eternal King,
Thy name we sing, while faith adores.

INDEX OF FIRST LINES OF PSALMS AND HYMNS.

(201)

PART SECOND.

FOR MORE PRIVATE USE

CONTAINING

I. WHAT IS RELIGION? II. BRIEF EXPOSITIONS. III. PRAYERS
FOR VARIOUS OCCASIONS. IV. FRIENDLY
ADVICES TO SEAMEN.

(203)

PART II.

WHAT IS RELIGION?

———◆———

THERE are many false religions in the world, which produce no happy change in our character; which exert no influence in promoting our happiness; and have no effect in preparing the soul for death and eternity.

The only true religion is that which is revealed by God in the Holy Bible. In all ages of the world, where this religion is truly and heartily embraced, it has shown its power in reforming the life, bringing the soul safely through all the afflictions of this world, and supporting it in the hour of death, with the cheering hope of a happy hereafter.

The religion of the Bible regards all men by nature as fallen sinful creatures.

AS by one man [Adam] sin entered into the world, and death by sin; and so death passed upon all men, for that all have sinned. Rom. v. 12. [See also the whole of this chapter.]

Behold I was shapen in iniquity: and in sin did my mother conceive me. Psalm li. 5.

The wicked are estranged from the womb: they go

astray as soon as they be born, speaking lies. Psalm
lviii. 3

For out of the heart proceed evil thoughts, murders,
adulteries, fornications, thefts, false-witness, blasphemies.
These are the things which defile a man.   Matt. xv. 19, 20.

How much more abominable and filthy is man which
drinketh iniquity like water !   Job xv. 16.

And God saw that the wickedness of man was great in
the earth, and that every imagination of the thoughts of
his heart was only evil continually.   Gen. vi. 5.

The Bible represents sin of all kinds as exposing the sinner to God's wrath.

BUT unto them that are contentious, and do not obey
the truth, but obey unrighteousness, indignation
and wrath, tribulation and anguish upon every soul of man
that doth evil.   Rom. ii. 8, 9.

God is angry with the wicked every day. Psalm vii. 11.

The wrath of God is revealed from heaven against all
ungodliness and unrighteousness of men.   Rom. i. 18.

The Lord shall send upon thee cursing, vexation and
rebuke, in all that thou settest thine hand unto for to do,
until thou be destroyed and until thou perish quickly;
because of the wickedness of thy doings, whereby thou
hast forsaken me.   Deut. xxviii. 20.

Upon the wicked he shall rain snares, fire and brimstone, and an horrible tempest : this shall be the portion
of their cup. Psalm xi. 6.

The wicked shall be cut off from the earth, and the
transgressors shall be rooted out of it.   Prov. ii. 22.

The face of the Lord is against them that do evil. 1
Pet. iii. 12.

That they all might be damned who believed not the
truth, but had pleasure in unrighteousness. 2 Thess. ii. 12.

The Lord Jesus shall be revealed from heaven with
his mighty angels in flaming fire, taking vengeance on
them that know not God and that obey not the gospel of

our Lord Jesus Christ; who shall be punished with ever-lasting destruction from the presence of the Lord and from the glory of his power. 2 Thess. i. 7—9.

Then shall he (Christ) say unto them on the left hand, Depart from me, ye cursed, into everlasting fire, pre-pared for the devil and his angels. Matt. xxv. 41.

But the fearful, and unbelieving, and the abominable, and murderers, and whoremongers, and sorcerers, and idolaters, and all liars, shall have their part in the lake which burneth with fire and brimstone : which is the second death.

The Bible represents sinners as unable to save themselves, and that all help must come from God.

O ISRAEL, thou hast destroyed thyself : but in me is thy help. Hosea xiii. 9.

Oh remember not against us former iniquities : let thy tender mercies speedily prevent us : for we are brought very low. Help us, O God of our salvation, for the glory of thy name, and deliver us and purge away our sins, for thy name's sake. Psalm lxxix. 8, 9.

Give us help from trouble : for vain is the help of man. Psalm lx. 11.

I will lift up mine eyes unto the hills from whence cometh my help. My help cometh from the Lord which made heaven and earth. Psalm cxxi. 1, 2.

God be merciful to me a sinner. Luke xviii. 13.

Let us come boldly unto the throne of grace, that we may obtain mercy and find grace to help in time of need. Heb. iv. 16.

The Bible sets forth Jesus Christ as the only Saviour of sinners.

THE Son of man is come to save that which was lost. Matt. xviii. 11.

God sent not his Son into the world to condemn the world ; but that the world through him might be saved. John iii. 17

Neither is there salvation in any other: for there is none other name under heaven given among men whereby we must be saved. Acts iv. 12.

Jesus saith unto him, I am the way, the truth, and the life: no man cometh unto the Father, but by me. John xiv. 6.

Him hath God exalted with his right hand to be a Prince and a Saviour, to give repentance to Israel and forgiveness of sin. Acts v. 31.

But we believe that through the grace of the Lord Jesus Christ we shall be saved. Acts xv. 11.

Wherefore he is able also to save them to the uttermost that come unto God by him, seeing he ever liveth to make intercession for them. Heb. vii. 25.

For God hath not appointed us to wrath, but to obtain salvation by our Lord Jesus Christ, who died for us. 1 Thess. v. 9.

Who his own self bare our sins in his own body on the tree, that we being dead to sins, should live unto righteousness: by whose stripes ye were healed. 1 Peter ii. 24.

The Bible represents the necessity of faith or belief in Christ, in order that we may be saved by him.

THIS is his commandment that we should believe on the name of his Son, Jesus Christ. 1 John iii. 23.

If thou shalt confess with thy mouth the Lord Jesus, and shalt believe in thy heart that God hath raised him from the dead, thou shalt be saved. For with the heart man believeth unto righteousness, and with the mouth confession is made unto salvation. Rom. x. 9, 10.

By grace are ye saved through faith, and that not of yourselves, it is the gift of God. Eph. ii. 8.

Verily, verily, I say unto you, He that heareth my word and believeth on him that sent me, hath everlasting life, and shall not come into condemnation; but is passed from death unto life. John v. 24.

For God so loved the world, that he gave his only begotten Son, that whosoever believeth in him should not perish, but have everlasting life. For God sent not his Son into the world to condemn the world : but that the world through him might be saved. He that believeth on him is not condemned ; but he that believeth not, is condemned already, because he hath not believed in the name of the only begotten Son of God. John iii. 16—18.

The Bible represents true repentance as necessary to salvation.

THAT they should repent and turn to God and do works meet for repentance. Acts xxvi. 20.

Repent and be converted, that your sins may be blotted out. Acts iii. 19.

He that covereth his sins shall not prosper ; but whoso confesseth and forsaketh them shall have mercy. Prov. xxviii. 13.

If we confess our sins, he is faithful and just to forgive us our sins, and to cleanse us from all unrighteousness. 1 John i. 9.

The Lord is nigh unto them that are of a broken heart ; and saveth such as be of a contrite spirit. Psalm xxxiv. 18.

The Bible teaches that where there is true repentance God will extend forgiveness.

LET the wicked forsake his way, and the unrighteous man his thoughts ; and let him return unto the Lord, and he will have mercy upon him, and to our God, for he will abundantly pardon. Isa. lv. 7.

I will be merciful to their unrighteousness, and their sins and their iniquities will I remember no more. Heb. viii. 12.

Come now, and let us reason together, saith the Lord : Though your sins be as scarlet, they shall be white as snow ; though they be red like crimson, they shall be as wool. Isa. i. 18.

Lord, thou art good, and ready to forgive ; and plen-

18 *

tcous in mercy unto all them that call upon thee.   Psalm
lxxxvi. 5.

The Bible teaches a religion that will lead to holy obedience.

FEAR God and keep his commandments, for this is the
whole duty of man.   Eccles. xii. 13.

Observe to do according to all the law; turn not from
it to the right hand, or to the left; that thou mayest prosper whithersoever thou goest.   Josh. i. 7.

Jesus said, If ye love me, keep my commandments—
He that hath my commandments, and keepeth them, he
it is that loveth me.   John xiv. 15, 21.

Whosoever shall break one of these least commandments, and shall teach men so, shall be called the least
in the kingdom of heaven.   Matt. v. 19.

Blessed are they that do his commandments, that they
may have a right to the tree of life, and may enter in
through the gates into the city.   Rev. xxii. 14.

The Bible teaches us to love and fear God.

LOVE the Lord your God, and serve him with all your
heart, and with all your soul.   Deut. xi. 13.

Thou shalt love the Lord thy God with all thine heart,
and with all thy soul, and with all thy might.   Deut.
vi. 5.

And we know that all things work together for good
to them that love God.   Rom. viii. 28.

The fear of the Lord is the beginning of wisdom.
Psalm cxi. 10.

I will give them one heart and one way, that they may
fear me for ever.   Jer. xxxii. 39.

Fear the Lord and depart from evil.   Prov. iii. 7.

Unto you that fear my name shall the Sun of righteousness arise with healing in his wings.   Mal. iv. 2.

The Bible leads the soul to hate sin and avoid temptation.

WHEREFORE I abhor myself and repent in dust
and ashes.   Job xlii. 6.

And they shall loathe themselves for the evils which they have committed, in all their abominations, Ezek. vi. 9.

If I have done iniquity, I will do no more. Job xxxiv. 32.

Wash you, make you clean; put away the evil of your doings from before mine eyes; cease to do evil, learn to do well. Isa. i. 16.

Wherefore, come out from among them, and be ye separate, saith the Lord, and touch not the unclean thing, and I will receive you. 2 Cor. vi. 17.

Abstain from all appearance of evil. 1 Thess. v. 22.

My son, if sinners entice thee, consent thou not. Prov. i. 10.

Blessed is the man that walketh not in the counsel of the ungodly, nor standeth in the way of sinners, nor sitteth in the seat of the scornful. Psalm i. 1.

The Bible teaches us to love the Word of God.

SEARCH the scriptures : for in them ye think ye have eternal life : and they are they which testify of me. John v. 39.

Oh, how love I thy law! it is my meditation all the day. Psalm cxix. 97.

How sweet are thy words unto my taste! yea, sweeter than honey to my mouth. Psalm cxix. 103.

Thy testimonies are wonderful, therefore doth my soul keep them. Psalm cxix. 129.

All scripture is given by inspiration of God, and is profitable for doctrine, for reproof, for correction, for instruction in righteousness ; that the man of God may be perfect, thoroughly furnished unto all good works. 2 Tim. iii. 16, 17.

The Bible enjoins it on men to pray.

I WILL therefore, that men pray everywhere, lifting up holy hands, without wrath and doubting. 1 Tim. ii. 8.

Evening, and morning, and at noon will I pray and cry aloud ; and he shall hear my voice. Psalm lv. 17.

Continuing instant in prayer. Rom. xii. 12.

Continue in prayer, and watch in the same with thanksgiving. Col. iv. 2.

But thou when thou prayest, enter into thy closet, and when thou hast shut thy door, pray to thy Father which is in secret ; and thy Father which seeth in secret shall reward thee openly. Matt. vi. 6.

If we ask anything according to his will, he heareth us. 1 John v. 14.

The Bible teaches us to be thankful to God.

IT is a good thing to give thanks unto the Lord, and to sing praises unto thy name, O most high : to show forth thy loving-kindness in the morning, and thy faithfulness every night. Psalm xcii. 1, 2.

In everything by prayer and supplication, with thanksgiving, let your requests be made known unto God. Phil. iv. 6.

Giving thanks always for all things unto God and the Father, in the name of our Lord Jesus Christ. Eph. v. 20.

Bless the Lord, O my soul ; and all that is within me, bless his holy name. Bless the Lord, O my soul, and forget not all his benefits ; who forgiveth all thine iniquities ; who healeth all thy diseases ; who redeemeth thy life from destruction ; who crowneth thee with loving-kindness, and tender mercies. Psalm ciii. 1—4.

The Bible teaches us to submit to God.

SUBMIT yourselves therefore to God. James iv. 7. Thy will be done. Matt. vi. 10.

The Lord gave, and the Lord hath taken away ; blessed be the name of the Lord. Job i. 21.

What ! shall we receive good at the hand of God, and shall we not receive evil ? Job ii. 10.

The Bible teaches us to forgive our enemies, and to return good for evil.

AND when ye stand praying, forgive, if ye have aught against any; that your Father also which is in heaven may forgive you your trespasses; but if ye do not forgive, neither will your Father which is in heaven forgive your trespasses. Mark xi. 25, 26.

Recompense to no man evil for evil.—Dearly beloved, avenge not yourselves, but rather give place unto wrath; for it is written, Vengeance is mine, I will repay, saith the Lord. Therefore if thine enemy hunger, feed him; if he thirst, give him drink; for in so doing thou shalt heap coals of fire on his head. Be not overcome of evil, but overcome evil with good, Rom. xii. 17, 19, 20, 21.

But I say unto you, Love your enemies, bless them that curse you, and pray for them which despitefully use you and persecute you. Matt. v. 44.

The Bible teaches us not to set our affections on this present world.

LOVE not the world, neither the things that are in the world. If any man love the world, the love of the Father is not in him. For all that is in the world, the lust of the flesh, and the lust of the eyes, and the pride of life, is not of the Father but is of the world. 1 John ii. 15.

Set your affections on things above, not on things on the earth. Col. iii. 2.

Let your conversation be without covetousness; and be content with such things as ye have. Heb. xiii. 5.

And seek not ye what ye shall eat, or what ye shall drink, neither be ye of doubtful mind. For all these things do the nations of the world seek after; and your Father knoweth that ye have need of these things. But rather seek ye the kingdom of God, and all these things shall be added unto you. Luke xii. 29—31.

The Bible teaches us to be examples to others in all good dispositions and conduct.

LET all bitterness, and wrath, and anger, and clamour, and evil-speaking, be put away from you, with all malice: and be ye kind one to another, tender-hearted, forgiving one another, even as God for Christ's sake hath forgiven you. Eph. iv. 31, 32.

Be thou an example of the believers in word, in conversation, in charity, in spirit, in faith, in purity. 1 Tim. iv. 12.

Let us walk honestly, as in the day, not in rioting and drunkenness, not in chambering and wantonness, not in strife and envying. Rom. xiii. 13.

If it be possible, as much as lieth in you, live peaceably with all men. Rom. xii. 18.

Let love be without dissimulation. Abhor that which is evil: cleave to that which is good. Be kindly affectioned one to another with brotherly love; in honour preferring one another. Not slothful in business; fervent in spirit; serving the Lord; rejoicing in hope; patient in tribulation; continuing instant in prayer; distributing to the necessity of saints; given to hospitality. Rejoice with them that do rejoice, and weep with them that weep. Rom. xii. 9—15.

As ye would that men should do to you, do ye also to them likewise. Luke vi. 31.

See that none render evil for evil, unto any man; but ever follow that which is good, both among yourselves and to all men. 1 Thess. v. 15.

But to do good and to communicate forget not; for with such sacrifices God is well pleased. Heb. xiii. 16.

Let none of you suffer as a murderer, or as a thief, or as an evil doer, or as a busy-body in other men's matters. 1 Peter iv. 15.

Do all things without murmurings and disputings; that ye may be blameless and harmless, the sons of God, without rebuke, in the midst of a crooked and perverse nation among whom ye shine as lights in the world. Phil. ii. 14, 15.

What doth the Lord require of thee, but to do justly, and to love mercy, and to walk humbly with thy God! Micah vi. 8.

Learn to do well : seek judgment, relieve the oppressed ; judge the fatherless ; plead for the widow. Is. i. 17.

Let your light so shine before men, that they may see your good works and glorify your father which is in heaven. Matt. v. 16.

The religion of the Bible supports in affliction and disarms death.

CHOOSING rather to suffer affliction with the people of God, than to enjoy the pleasures of sin for a season. Heb. xi. 25.

Many are the afflictions of the righteous ; but the Lord delivereth him out of them all. Psalm xxxiv. 19.

For our light affliction which is but for a moment, worketh for us a far more exceeding and eternal weight of glory. 2 Cor. iv. 17.

Mark the perfect man and behold the upright : for the end of that man is peace. Psalm xxxvii. 37.

Precious in the sight of the Lord is the death of his saints. Psalm cxvi. 15.

For to me to live is Christ, and to die is gain. Phil. i. 21.

And I heard a voice from heaven saying unto me, Write, Blessed are the dead which die in the Lord from henceforth ; Yea, saith the Spirit, that they may rest from their labours, and their works do follow them. Rev. xiv. 13.

O death, where is thy sting? O grave, where is thy victory? The sting of death is sin, and the strength of sin is the law ; but thanks be to God which giveth us the victory through our Lord Jesus Christ. 1 Cor. xv. 56, 57.

The religion of the Bible secures our resurrection from the
 grave and our happiness in heaven.

FOR we know that if our earthly house of this tabernacle were dissolved, we have a building of God, a
house not made with hands, eternal in the heavens. 2
Cor. v. 1.

For if we believe that Jesus died and rose again, even
so them also which sleep in Jesus will God bring with
him. 1 Thess.-iv. 14.

For this corruptible must put on incorruption, and this
mortal must put on immortality. So when this corruptible shall have put on incorruption, and this mortal shall
have put on immortality, then shall be brought to pass
the saying that is written, Death is swallowed up in victory. 1 Cor. xv. 54.

And the sea gave up the dead which were in it. Rev.
xx. 13.

Beloved, now are we the sons of God, and it doth not
yet appear what we shall be, but we know that when he
shall appear, we shall be like him, for we shall see him as
he is. 1 John iii. 2.

Blessed be the God and Father of our Lord Jesus
Christ, which according to his abundant mercy hath begotten us again unto a lively hope, by the resurrection of
Jesus Christ from the dead, to an inheritance, incorruptible and undefiled, and that fadeth not away, reserved in
heaven for you. 1 Peter i. 3, 4.

In my Father's house are many mansions; if it were
not so, I would have told you. I go to prepare a place
for you. And if I go and prepare a place for you, I will
come again and receive you unto myself, that where I am
there ye may be also. John xiv. 2, 3.

Thou wilt show-me the path of life; in thy presence
is fulness of joy; at thy right hand there are pleasures
for evermore. Psalm xvi. 11.

And God shall wipe away all tears from their eyes; and

there shall be no more death; neither sorrow nor crying, neither shall there be any more pain; for the former things are passed away.   Rev. xxi. 4.

BRIEF EXPOSITION OF THE TEN COMMANDMENTS.

I. Thou shalt have no other gods before me.

This commandment requires us to know and acknowledge God to be the only true God, and our God, and to worship and glorify him accordingly;

And it forbids the denying and not worshipping and glorifying the true God as God and our God; and the giving that worship and glory to any other which is due to him alone.

II. Thou shalt not make unto thee any graven image, or any likeness of anything that is in heaven above, or that is in the earth beneath, or that is in the water under the earth; thou shalt not bow down thyself to them, nor serve them; for I the Lord thy God, am a jealous God, visiting the iniquity of the fathers upon the children, unto the third and fourth generation of them that hate me; and showing mercy unto thousands of them that love me and keep my commandments.

This commandment requires the receiving, observing and keeping pure and entire, all such religious worship and ordinances as God has appointed in his word;

And it forbids the worshipping of God by images, or any other way not appointed in his word.

III. Thou shalt not take the name of the Lord thy

19

God in vain; for the Lord will not hold him guiltless that taketh his name in vain.

This commandment requires the holy and reverent use of God's names, titles, attributes, ordinances, word, and works;

And it forbids all profaning or abusing of anything whereby God maketh himself known. And however the breakers of this commandment may escape punishment from men, yet the Lord our God will not suffer them to escape his righteous judgment.

IV. Remember the Sabbath day to keep it holy. Six days shalt thou labour and do all thy work; but the seventh day is the Sabbath of the Lord thy God; in it thou shalt not do any work, thou, nor thy son, nor thy daughter, thy man-servant, nor thy maid-servant, nor thy cattle, nor thy stranger, that is within thy gates; for in six days the Lord made heaven and earth, the sea, and all that in them is, and rested the seventh day; wherefore the Lord blessed the Sabbath day and hallowed it.

This commandment requires the keeping holy to God such set times as he hath appointed in his word; expressly one whole day in seven to be a holy Sabbath to himself;

And it forbids the omission or careless performance of the duties required, and the profaning the day by idleness, or doing that which is in itself sinful, or by unnecessary thoughts, words, or works, about our worldly employments or recreations. Thus the Sabbath is to be sanctified by a

holy resting all that day, even from such worldly
employments and recreations as are lawful on
other days ; and spending the whole time in the
public and private exercises of God's worship, except so much as is to be taken up in the works of
necessity and mercy.

V. Honour thy father and thy mother that thy days
may be long upon the land which the Lord thy God
giveth thee

This commandment requires the preserving the
honour, and performing the duties belonging to
every one in their several places and relations, as
superiors, inferiors, or equals ;

And it forbids the neglecting of, or doing any
thing against, the honour and duty which belongeth
to every one in their several places and relations.

VI. Thou shalt not kill.

This commandment requires all lawful endeav-
ours to preserve our own life and the life of others ;

And it forbids the taking away of our own life,
or the life of our neighbour unjustly, or whatsoever tendeth thereunto.

VII. Thou shalt not commit adultery.

This commandment requires the preservation
of our own and our neighbour's chastity, in heart,
speech, and behaviour ;

And it forbids all unchaste thoughts, words and
actions.

VIII. Thou shalt not steal.

This commandment requires the lawful procuring and furthering the wealth and outward estate of ourselves and others;

And it forbids whatsoever doth or may unjustly hinder our own, or our neighbour's wealth or outward estate.

IX. Thou shalt not bear false witness against thy neighbour.

This commandment requires the maintaining and promoting of truth between man and man, and of our own and our neighbour's good name, especially in witness-bearing;

And it forbids whatsoever is prejudicial to truth, or injurious to our own, or our neighbour's good name.

X. Thou shalt not covet thy neighbour's house, thou shalt not covet thy neighbour's wife, nor his man-servant, nor his maid-servant, nor his ox, nor his ass, nor any thing that is thy neighbour's.

This commandment requires full contentment with our own condition, with a right and charitable frame of spirit towards our neighbour, and all that is his;

And it forbids all discontentment with our own estate, envying or grieving at the good of our neighbour, and all inordinate motions or affections to any thing that is his.

A BRIEF EXPOSITION OF THE LORD'S PRAYER.

1. Our Father which art in heaven.

This teaches us to draw near to God with all holy reverence and confidence, as children to a father, able and ready to help us: and that we should pray with and for others.

2. Hallowed be thy name.

In this we pray, that God would enable us and others to glorify him in all that whereby he makes himself known, and that he would dispose all things to his own glory.

3. Thy kingdom come.

In this we pray that Satan's kingdom may be destroyed, and that the kingdom of grace may be advanced, ourselves and others brought into it, and kept in it, and that the kingdom of glory may be hastened.

4. Thy will be done in earth, as it is in heaven

In this we pray, that God, by his grace, would make us able and willing to know, obey, and submit to his will in all things, as the angels do in heaven.

5. Give us this day our daily bread.

In this we pray, that of God's free gift we may receive a competent portion of the good things of this life, and enjoy his blessing with them.

19 *

6. And forgive us our debts, as we forgive our debtors.

In this we pray, that God, for Christ's sake, would freely pardon all our sins; which we are the rather encouraged to ask, because by his grace we are enabled from the heart to forgive others.

7. And lead us not into temptation, but deliver us from evil.

In this we pray, that God would either keep us from being tempted to sin, or support and deliver us when we are tempted.

8. For thine is the kingdom, and the power, and the glory for ever, Amen.

In this we are taught to take our encouragement in prayer from God only, and in our prayers to praise him, ascribing kingdom, power, and glory to him; and in testimony of our desire and assurance to be heard, we say, Amen.

PRAYERS FOR VARIOUS OCCASIONS,

WHICH MAY BE USED IN PUBLIC, SOCIAL, AND PRIVATE WORSHIP.

A Prayer for Penitence.

HAVE mercy upon us, O God, according to thy loving-kindness; according unto the multitude of thy tender mercies, blot out our transgressions. Wash us thoroughly from our iniquity and cleanse us from our sin. For we acknowledge our transgressions and our sins are ever before us. Behold we were shapen in iniquity and conceived in sin. Hide thou thy face from our sins and blot out all our iniquities. Create in us clean hearts, and renew a right spirit within us. Cast us not away from thy presence and take not thy Holy Spirit from us. Then will we teach transgressors thy ways, and sinners shall be converted unto thee. The sacrifices of God are a broken spirit; a broken and a contrite heart, O God, thou wilt not despise. Accept these, our humble confessions, for Christ's sake, Amen.

A Prayer for Pardoning Mercy.

MOST holy God, as sinners we need forgiveness. From our early youth we have sinned against thee in thought, word, and deed. May we have the blessedness of those whose transgression is forgiven, whose sin is covered, unto whom the Lord imputeth not iniquity. Apply to us the cleansing blood of the cross, and through it may we have redemption, even the forgiveness of sins, according to the riches of thy grace. So may we be justified and sanctified, that sin shall no longer be suffered to dwell in our hearts, or bring us into condemnation; and this we ask for His sake, who came into the world to put away sin by the sacrifice of himself; and to him shall be all the praise, Amen.

A Prayer for Light and Knowledge.

O THOU who art light and in whom there is no darkness at all, shine into our hearts, and give us the light of the knowledge of the glory of God in the face of Jesus Christ. Reveal to us the excellency of thy character and government, especially as thou hast made thyself known in the redemption of the world by Jesus Christ. May thy word be a lamp to our feet and a light to our path, that we may at all times know what thou wouldst have us to do. May all the blessed doctrines and precepts of thy word be clearly understood, and heartily believed and practised by us, that we may no longer err and stray from thy ways. May we know also our own true character and condition, that we may not think more highly of ourselves than we ought to think, or flatter ourselves with hopes which are not well founded and sure. Pity and pardon our former neglect to improve our privileges, as learners at the feet of Jesus; and now may we be so taught of God, that we may daily increase in wisdom and in understanding; which we ask for Christ's sake, Amen.

A Prayer for Decision in Religion.

O RIGHTEOUS God, who would have men everywhere to repent and turn to thee, may we no longer halt between two opinions; but resolve, that, whatever others may do, we will serve the

Lord. We know that we cannot serve two masters, and must choose between thee and the world. Enable us, we beseech thee, with a true and sincere heart, to take thee as our portion, and from henceforth renounce the world, the flesh, and the devil. Let the time past suffice us to have done the will of the flesh, and from this good hour may we give our hearts to thee, that we may love, serve, and honour thee, as our only Lord and Master. Thou, Lord, hast bought us with a price; we are no longer our own; and as thou hast said, Son give me thy heart, forbid that we should any longer love the world, or the things which are in the world. May we henceforth be the disciples of the meek and lowly Jesus; be firm in our purpose to renounce the companionship of the wicked, however they may deride us; and be earnest in seeking thy love and favour, and the salvation of our immortal souls. Which we ask for Christ's sake, Amen.

A Prayer for Protection against Temptation.

O GOD, thou, who knowest all things, art acquainted with our weaknesses and infirmities, and the danger we are in of being carried away by the enticements of sinners. We have evil hearts of unbelief, which cause us to depart from God; and are subject to easily besetting sins, which cannot be overcome in our own strength. Pity the weakness of our resolutions, for even when we would do good, evil is present with us, and prevails against us.   When surrounded by wicked companions, and exposed to their profane and filthy conversation, may we not be led astray by their example, but flee to thee for help.   And, O most gracious God, when the temptations of a foreign port assail us, and we see our shipmates led astray by the gamblers, the intemperate, and the licentious, may we stand aloof, and refuse their enticements, taught as we are by thy holy word that the path of sin, however pleasing to the sense, leadeth down to the chambers of death.   Under thy merciful protection we place ourselves, that we may be kept in all our ways, and preserved unto thy heavenly glory, for Christ's sake, Amen.

A Prayer against Infidelity.

O GOD of salvation, who hast assured us that only he that believeth in Jesus shall be saved, confirm our hearts in the constant belief of the truth of thy word.   While others cast away the fear of God and the wholesome restraints of thy law, may we receive the religion of thy holy gospel as the truth come down from heaven, and hold it closely to our hearts.   O God, shine into our minds and hearts with convincing evidence, and may all infidel thoughts concerning thee and thy Son, Jesus Christ, be resisted, and overcome.

Unto whom shall we go but unto thee, for thou hast the words of eternal life? Thou art the fountain of life, and all other resorts are but broken cisterns which can hold no water. Lord, we believe, help thou our unbelief, for the sake of thy well beloved Son, our Saviour, Amen.

General Thanksgiving.

O MOST bountiful God, who, of thy great goodness, hast endowed us with bodies fearfully and wonderfully made, and with souls susceptible of endless happiness, we render to thee our hearty thanks. We thank thee that thou hast given fruitfulness to the earth that it may bring forth food for man and beast, and that thou hast spread out the sea as a great highway. We thank thee that all the works which thou hast created are good, and useful, and beautiful; and that they remind us of thy wisdom, skill, and beneficence. We thank thee that, even in our sinful apostasy, thou hast not left us without hope; but in the fulness of time didst send thy Son into the world to seek and save the lost. We thank thee that he humbled himself in taking upon him the form of a servant; that he went about doing good; that he patiently endured the wicked enmity of men; that he offered himself as a sacrifice for sin; and that, having finished his work, he rose from the dead, ascended into heaven, and now ever liveth to make intercession for us. We thank thee for thy preserving goodness and forbearance toward us; and most especially do we thank thee if thou hast brought us back from our wanderings, restored us to thy favour, and made us partakers of that good hope in Christ which shall never fail us. To Father, Son, and Holy Ghost, we render thanks and praise, both now and for ever, Amen.

A Prayer in Time of Peril.

ALMIGHTY God, who rulest the raging of the sea when the waves thereof arise, we would direct our supplications to thee in this time of peril. While we would employ every means of safety, and courageously perform our duty, we would not forget that human strength is insignificant, and human skill may prove of no avail. Thou couldst overwhelm us in a moment, and cast us helpless on the mighty deep; but O Lord most merciful, look upon us in our extremity, rebuke the winds and the waves, and send us speedy deliverance. If it be thy holy will, may we survive this danger, and be brought in safety to our destined port; but if it be thy will that we are to be called hence, then bid us come to thee on the water; sweeten the pain of our departure, and through the infinite merits of our Lord and Saviour, prepare us for thy heavenly kingdom, where there shall be no more peril, no more death, but everlasting security and happiness. And thine shall be the glory for ever, Amen.

A Prayer during Sickness on Shipboard.

O THOU from whom we have received our life, in thy wise providence, it has pleased thee to commission disease to visit our vessel, that we may be reminded of our mortality and turn our thoughts heavenward. While threatening sickness has laid low some of our companions, and may assail us also; we implore thy gracious interference that the disease may be stayed, and health restored. Thou canst kill and make alive, and although our sins have justly provoked thy judgments, yet withhold thy hand and let mercy prevail. May none of our companions be summoned hence in an unconverted state. If thou hast appointed them to death, may they first experience repentance towards God and faith in our Lord Jesus Christ, so that death may prove to them great gain. If thou shalt be pleased to give efficacy to the remedies employed, and restore them to health, awaken in their hearts devout gratitude to thee from whom cometh every good and perfect gift. Which we ask for Christ's sake, Amen.

Thanksgiving for Deliverance from Peril.

O THOU who art the hearer of prayer, we have cried unto thee in the time of danger and thou hast sent us speedy deliverance. When innumerable dangers surrounded us, thou didst show thyself mighty to save. We would not as-

20

cribe our safety to our own skill and courage, but to that Almighty hand which aided our feeble efforts, calming our fears, and bidding us be of good cheer. Most merciful God, suffer us not to be unmindful of thy goodness which has so remarkably appeared in our behalf. Henceforth may we trust thee, and be not faithless, but believing. May we not forget that, in our peculiar calling as seamen, we are exposed to many dangers. The tempests may beat on us, fire may consume us, provisions may fail, a rock-bound coast may endanger, our vessel may prove unseaworthy and founder; but in every extremity thou art all-sufficient, and to thee, therefore, would we go under all circumstances, and prove thy goodness and mercy. And to thy name shall be all the praise through Christ Jesus, the Lord, Amen.

A Prayer on the Eve of Battle.

O GOD, who art our shield in the day of battle, and canst alone be our safeguard when sudden death threatens on every hand, we commit ourselves to thy merciful protection. Every bullet has its commission from thee, and strikes according to thy direction, and not by chance. As we are here to guard our country's honour and safety, we pray that we may be inspired with becoming courage; and, however great the peril, be prepared to perform our duty faithfully, and without any shrinking of fear. Amidst the noise and smoke of battle, may we maintain our steadiness, and remember that our lives are in thy hand. If any of us should fall, may our souls be safe through thy mercy; or if we should be wounded, may we be patient and submissive. If it be thy holy will, grant that our efforts be crowned with victory, and may it be accomplished with as little bloodshed as possible. O God of battles, in the hour of conflict, forget not us, nor suffer us to forget thee. With us it is a time of need; with thee may it be a time of merciful deliverance, and may we yet live to praise thee. All which we ask for our Redeemer's sake. Amen.

A Prayer after Battle.

O GRACIOUS and ever present God, we have called upon thee and thou hast heard us. Although some of our comrades have fallen, and others are sorely wounded, the shield of thy protection has been around us, and we are yet in the land of the living to praise thee. How fearful the scenes through which we have just passed, and yet thou hast not left us to dishonour ourselves by forsaking our posts, or shrinking from duty! There has been but a step between us and death, and yet how marvellous has been our preservation! Let there be among us no vain boasting, but a spirit of devout gratitude to God. We would

call upon our souls, and all that is within us to
bless and magnify thy holy name.   Grant to our
wounded comrades thy gracious presence, and in
the midst of their sufferings soothe their feelings,
mitigate their pains, and restore them again to
soundness of body.   Prepare them for thy will
whatever that will may be, and vouchsafe to us a
thankful heart, that in all future life we may recall to mind the favour which thou hast shown to
us on this occasion.   And unto the Father, the
Son, and the Holy Spirit, shall be the praise, world
without end, Amen.

A Prayer when outward bound.

THY providence, O Lord, is everywhere the same
on the land and on the mighty deep, and to
that providence we would now commit ourselves.
While in the pursuit of lawful business, we leave
port, we commend to thy fatherly care our relatives
and friends whom we leave behind, and we pray
thee ever to have them in thy holy keeping.   May
they find thee a safe tower to which, in every
danger, they may betake themselves, and may no
plague come nigh their dwelling.   Through thy
favour may we all again meet together in peace,
and present to thee our common thanksgivings.
And may we, who are now about to enter on the
wide sea, be prospered in our undertaking.   Thou
who commandest the winds and waves, send us on

our voyage with thy blessing. May our vessel prove staunch, our officers skilful, and our men faithful to duty. Let not the threatening tempest assail us, or the raging waves endanger us; but grant us favouring winds that our voyage may be speedily and safely accomplished. Then will we praise the Lord for his goodness and for his wonderful works to the children of men; these mercies we ask for Christ's sake, Amen.

A Prayer on entering Port.

OUR Father who art in heaven, thou rulest over all, and thy footsteps are on the sea. Blessed be thy name, thou hast favoured us with thy presence, and after tossing on the mighty waters we are permitted, by thy good providence, to enter our destined port. In the day and night watches thou hast been our keeper, and no serious calamity has befallen us. For this we would heartily thank thee. No tempest has shattered our barque, no fatal collision has occurred, no fire or water has gained the mastery over us, and the deep has not been made our burial place. May we keep in lively remembrance thy providence over us; may we truly confess and forsake our sins, and flee for refuge to that gracious Redeemer who has died for us. Trusting alone in his merits, may we, when the voyage of life is over, enter into that heavenly port, where the storms of life shall no

20 *

longer assail us, and where we shall find rest to our souls. Which we ask for his name's sake, Amen.

A Prayer when ship-wrecked and destitute.

O MOST righteous and merciful God, without whose will, not a sparrow falleth to the ground, and who in thy gracious providence dost furnish food to the young ravens when they cry; it is by thy will that we are now in straits and difficulties, from which thy mercy alone can relieve us. Painful as our afflictions are, they are not as grievous as our sins have deserved. Thou hast spared our lives when in peril, and given us still longer time for repentance; and although now we are destitute and helpless, we would look to thee who hast assured us that we shall not seek thee in vain. Graciously strengthen our feeble frames, provide from thy fulness the things which are necessary for our support and comfort, raise us up friends to succour us, and send us speedy deliverance. Pity us in our low state, for we are but dust; and let not thy just anger fall heavily upon us. For the past we praise thee, and for the present and future we would trust thee, confiding both soul and body to thy fatherly care. Hear the voice of our supplication for Christ's sake, Amen.

A Prayer under a Sense of Sin.

O THOU who art of purer eyes than to look on sin, have mercy upon us who have lived so long in transgression, regardless of consequences, and without the fear of God. Hard and impenitent have been our hearts, and alike indifferent have we been to the mercies and judgments of the Lord. But now, O Lord, we begin to see the greatness of our guilt, and the fearful dangers to which it exposes us. We have sinned against thee from our youth up, and our iniquities are more in number than we can reckon. And oh! how aggravated they have been, committed against so good and merciful a God! It would be just in thee to condemn us and cast us out for ever from thy presence; but O most merciful God, reward us not according to our iniquities, neither bring us into judgment, for we cannot answer thee for one of a thousand of our sins. Give us a sincere and godly sorrow, that we may not only heartily confess our sins, but, by thy grace, forsake them. We would turn our eyes to the cross of Jesus Christ, and see there the Lamb of God offered in sacrifice for the sins of the world. While we sorrowfully cry, God be merciful to us sinners, may we be enabled to see, how thou canst be both merciful and just in the forgiveness of our sins. Cleanse away our deep depravity, take away our enmity, restore to us thy love and favour, and for the sake of Jesus Christ, the only Redeemer of lost men, make us new creatures, who shall hereafter live godly, righteous, and sober lives. Which we ask for Christ's sake, Amen.

A Prayer before going to Sleep.

O LORD, thou who never slumberest, may thy watchful eyes ever be upon us. Grant unto us, at this time, peaceful and refreshening sleep, and guard us from all the dangers of the night-watches. Keep us from sudden alarms and preserve us from sudden death. When we lie down, and when we rise up, may we still be with thee, and feel confident that thou wilt never leave or forsake us. We ask it for Christ's sake, Amen.

A Prayer on Awaking from Sleep.

MERCIFUL God, we have laid ourselves down and slept, and awaked again, for thou didst sustain us. For this mercy, we devoutly thank thee, for thou art our keeper; may we now engage in our active duties with fresh spirit, and may all our waking thoughts and actions be such as thou wilt approve. We ask it for Christ's sake, Amen.

BRIEF EXPOSITIONS OF PASSAGES OF SCRIPTURE.

Luke xxiii. 34. " Father forgive them, for they know not what they do."

THIS was the prayer of the blessed Jesus when he hung upon the cross. Surrounded by his murderers, who were unfeelingly mocking his dying pangs, he cherished no feeling of revenge; he did not wish any punishment to overtake them; but earnestly prayed that they might be forgiven. Father, forgive them!

Now this Jesus is set forth as our example, that we should follow in his steps. If we would be his disciples, the same mind that dwelt in him must dwell in us. The spirit of wicked men is the spirit of revenge. They would take the law in their own hands, and visit with punishment those who do them any wrong. Their passions are aroused; they regard the offender with bitter hatred; and nothing they long so much for as to make him suffer. They not only refuse to do him any kindness, but rejoice when any calamity overtakes him. The anger which is roused within them not only leads to profane cursing, but to fighting and often to murder. Alas! this is not the spirit of Christ. He did not consider it unmanly to do good to his enemies, and to pray for them that despitefully used him; and he has enjoined upon us to render good for evil, and if our enemy hunger to feed him, and if he be thirsty to give him drink. This is a godlike temper, and is not only pleasing to God, but brings far greater peace of mind than a revengeful spirit. It is easier to overcome an enemy by kindness than by hatred; and grievously as our fellow men may sin against us, it is better to pray for them than to curse them. If we forgive not our fellow-men their trespasses, neither will God forgive us our trespasses. He mercifully forbears with us, and we should forbear with one another.

Luke xviii. 13. God be merciful to me a sinner.

THIS was the heartfelt prayer of the poor publican. He felt his sins to be grievous, and so far from offering any excuse for them, he smote upon his breast; would not so much as lift up his eyes to heaven; confessed that he was a sinner, and implored the divine mercy. Now this man was not a sinner above all others; perhaps he was better than thousands around him who showed no concern for their souls. God, however, had enlightened his mind; he had an insight into his own heart, and then he saw how great a sinner he was, and how certainly he must perish unless God pitied and pardoned. It is so now. Sinners are not troubled at their situation, because they have so blinded their minds and hardened their hearts, that they really do not know how great their danger is. If the Spirit once arouse them and pour light into their minds, they are no longer unconcerned. They tremble as the sins of their past life rise up before them; they feel that they are standing on the brink of ruin, that God is angry with them, and that their souls are in danger of perishing. Then they cry out, What must I do to be saved? Happy are they who are thus awakened. Their danger is no greater than it was before, but now they see it and wish to escape from it. A seaman may be swimming in the ocean; he may be enjoying himself, although there is a voracious shark making towards him; he has no fear, because he does not see his danger; but let him once see the monster approaching him, and how loudly will he cry for help! There is hope for a sinner when he sees his spiritual danger, for God is merciful, and they that call upon him for salvation through Jesus Christ shall not be disappointed. Behold the Lamb of God, ye heavy laden sinners, for it is he who taketh away sin, and who kindly says to the supplicant, Be of good cheer, thy sins are forgiven thee.

Proverbs xiv. 9.   Fools make a mock at sin.

SIN is too serious an evil to be made a jest of. It is the cause of all the misery which exists in our world. Had there been no sin, this world would have been a paradise, and pure happiness would have dwelt in every heart. Now what wretchedness do we everywhere see! What evil passions, what enmity, what poverty, what theft, profanity, intemperance, licentiousness ; what sickness, pain, and death ! and will any be so hardened as to make a mock at sin ? Shall we hear poor wretched men recounting their wicked deeds with triumph ? Shall they turn the blessed Bible into ridicule ? Shall they be merry at the expense of religion ? Shall they glory in being esteemed more reckless and hardened against God than their companions ? Surely if they thus make a mock at sin, they must be fools. Would not he be a fool who would laugh when his own house was burning, or his own children dying ? and is not he a fool who can sport with sin which is defiling his heart, separating him from the friendship of God, and closing the gates of heaven against him ? The souls of the lost never make a mock at sin, for they feel the evil of it in their everlasting perdition, and when the wicked, who, while they lived, neither feared God nor regarded man, come to a dying hour, they feel that sin is too serious an evil to be trifled with. Of all dooms, that of the mocker is the most fearful. The sin that he laughed at, will be like fire in his bones

Flee therefore the company of such fools and madmen, and ever remember that if sin had not been the greatest evil, the Son of God would not have come into our world to suffer and die that he might free man from its curse.

Isaiah i. 18. Come now and let us reason together, saith the Lord; though your sins be as scarlet, they shall be as white as snow; though they be red like crimson, they shall be as wool.

HOW gracious are these words! The most high God condescends to reason with the sinner, to persuade him, that his sins are not so numerous and grievous that they cannot be pardoned. The sinner, when convinced by the Holy Spirit of his lost and ruined state, is apt to cry out, Oh, I have sinned so long and sinned so fearfully, that there is no hope for me; God will never pardon me. And who has told you so, poor sinner? It is surely not God, for he has assured us in his word, that if we sincerely repent and believe in Jesus we shall be saved. The devil who has all your life long tempted you to sin, telling you there was no danger, would now drive you to de-

21

spair, by telling you that you have sinned away your day of grace, and that there is now no hope. Believe him not. Though your sins are of a scarlet and crimson dye, the Lord Jesus can wash you from them and give you a clean heart. And yet remember that this is no encouragement for you to go on in sin. There is no pardon for the impenitent. If you love sin too well to part with it, God will lift his hand and swear you shall not enter into his rest. If you take sin, you must take also its consequences, and these are misery here, and eternal misery hereafter. But if you freely confess and forsake your sins, God is faithful and just to forgive your sins and cleanse you from all unrighteousness.

Psalm xlvi. 1.   A very present help in trouble.

TROUBLE and affliction are the lot of all. They are the bitter fruits of sin. How many are the forms in which they assail us, and how inadequate is our strength to bear the burden! Enemies rise up and contrive to injure us; we are deprived of our property; friends prove false; our hopes are disappointed; sickness afflicts our bodies; our dearest earthly relatives die; and the recollection of our sins, and the fear of punishment disturb our peace; and sometimes our troubles come so suddenly and in such numbers, that we are ready to despair of deliverance. Those who have no God to flee to, in these dark hours, are greatly to be pitied. They resort to means of relief, which only aggravate their misery. Some strive to drown their trouble by intemperance, or by mingling with wild and wicked company; and not a few, driven to despair, deprive themselves of life by their own hand, and thus complete their misery by rushing into the presence of an angry God unprepared. The christian has a better remedy when overwhelmed with distress. He can go to his heavenly Father, who is pitiful and kind, and will not refuse to hear the cry of the distressed. He is a very present help in trouble. He has both the power and the will to soothe our sorrows, relieve our burdens, and send a calm, sweet peace into our hearts. Jesus Christ has a fellow feeling for us, and is afflicted in all our afflictions. His invitation is, Come unto me, and I will give you rest. It is necessary that we should be afflicted, that we may be reminded that we are sinful and mortal, and that this world is not our home; but how blessed is it to be supported under our trials, and to find that our Saviour can turn them into real blessings! Let us go therefore to him in every time of trouble, and pray that he would remove it, or graciously enable us to endure with patience, in view of that heavenly world where there shall be no more distress.

John xv. 13.   Greater love hath no man than this, that a man lay down his life for his friends.

HOW true is this! We may do much to show our friendship for others.   We may sacrifice time and property, and present ease, for their benefit.   We may defend them when slandered, nurse them when sick, share with them our last loaf, and encounter much danger to rescue them. The last and the greatest act of friendship is not only to risk our lives for them, but actually to die in their stead.   How few have been found to go so far as this, and lay down their lives for their friends!   Every one would applaud such a case as this, and exclaim, What noble self-denial!   But even such an example as this would be nothing in comparison with what Christ has done for us. "God commendeth his love toward us in that, while we were sinners, Christ died for us."   Yes, while we were sinners; and therefore, while we were enemies; while we were opposing him, doing the things which were displeasing to him, and re- fusing to reverence him as our Ruler, and love him as our Saviour; when we were ungrateful and unworthy sinners, Jesus died for us !   Oh, was ever love like this ?   The Son of God came down from heaven; he took on him the nature of man that he might dwell with us, and instruct and comfort us; and then when we rebelled against him and refused to return from our wanderings, he pitied us still, and as a last, great proof of his love, he offered up his life, to reconcile us to God. For such amazing love as this we should be ready to give up everything for Christ, and for the rest of our lives devote ourselves to his honour and glory.

John iii. 3.   Jesus answered and said unto him, Verily, verily, I say unto thee, Except a man be born again, he cannot see the kingdom of God

THIS was the language of Jesus to one of the chief men among the Jews, and from the strong and solemn manner in which it is expressed, we may regard it as containing a very important truth. Many will say, with Nicodemus, How can this be? What does it mean, to be born agam? The simple meaning of it is, that every one, who would enter into the kingdom of heaven, must first experience a change of heart and life, which will show that he has become a different person. Before this change, every one is destitute of love to God. He loves the world, he loves earthly pleasures, and has no desires beyond his present gratification. He dislikes God's holy law and hates to be restrained by it, because it is a holy law and forbids all sin. In all his actions and feelings, he shows that he has no love for his Maker. He seldom

21 *

thinks of him; he may fear him as a Judge, but does not draw nigh to him as a Father. He never worships God with pleasure, and has no true heart to pray unto him and to glorify him. He rather wishes there was no God to call him to an account for his sins. He sees nothing pleasing in religion, but rather treats it with neglect and contempt. He loves to indulge himself in sin, and makes no effort to live a holy life. Thus every man by nature is without God, without Christ, and without a religious hope. He lives in this world as if he was to live here for ever, and makes no preparation for death and eternity. When, however, God's mighty Spirit convinces him of his sin and danger, and shows him his helplessness; and when he at length directs him to Christ as the only Saviour; when he not only reveals his sinful heart to him, but enables him to flee to Christ for mercy, then a great change comes over him, old things pass away, and all things become new. Then he sees with new eyes his great guilt and danger; religion becomes to him the most important concern; God is looked up to with love and reverence; sin is regarded as the greatest evil, and every effort is made to lead a new life. The things he hated once he now loves, and what he once sinfully loved he now hates. He has become a new creature, he has been born again, and every one sees what a great change there is in his whole conduct. Now he prays;

now he lives to God and for eternity, and so far from practising his old sins, he hates and avoids them. Now if such a change is necessary before we can be saved, and if we cannot change our own hearts, we should earnestly beseech God for Christ's sake to make us new creatures

---

Proverbs xiii. 20. A companion of fools shall be destroyed.

BY fools are here meant, such as say in their heart there is no God, such as make a mock at sin, or in other words, such as despise religion, make it the subject of their jests, neglect the care of their souls, live in wickedness, and refuse to believe that after death comes the judgment. Surely it is the height of folly for an immortal creature who is accountable to God for his deeds, thus to feel and thus to act.

To be a companion of such, does not mean that we are never to be found where such men are, for this is often impossible. We may be in the same ship, and in the same mess with such men, when we cannot escape from their company. But it means to like and seek their society; to choose them as our friends, and to take a part in their evil doings. This makes us their companions, and whatever awaits them, awaits us. If they are to be destroyed, so will we be; if God's anger falls on them, we shall not escape. It is said, a man is known by the company he keeps, and it is equally true, that if we prefer the company of the wicked, we shall have a wicked man's reward. Let every one ask himself the question, who are my chosen companions? Do I like and choose to be found in the society of the profane, the intemperate, and the licentious? Do I enter heartily into their disorderly and wicked frolics? Do I follow them, when in port, to drinking and gambling houses and hotels? Then surely I am in the same condemnation, and when God cuts them off, he will destroy me also. The only way of safety is to shun their bad example, and resist the temptations which prove their ruin.

Haggai i. 5. Now, therefore, thus saith the Lord of hosts, Consider your ways.

THE merchant and tradesman watch the course of business; examine and compare their accounts; and carefully look into the state of their affairs, that they may know how things go with them. If in matters where only money is concerned, it is wise and prudent to consider our ways, how much more so where our eternal interests are concerned! God regards it as important, for "thus saith the Lord of hosts, Consider your ways." It would be well every day and more than once a day, to put such questions as these to ourselves; Am I living as an immortal and accountable creature should live? Am I endeavouring to keep God's commandments? What is the great object I am pursuing? is it merely to prosper in this world, or is it to be prepared for another? Or on the other hand, am I a careless and impenitent sinner? Do I habitually commit sins of thought, word and deed, without fear and without sorrow? Am I living here as if I were to live here for ever, and as if there was no death, no heaven, no hell? Is my course a good one, and will it be profitable in the end? These and such like questions we should ask of our own hearts and honestly answer. It will do us no harm to consider our ways, if we should find them to be such as our consciences can approve; and it may do us good to know if our course is a bad one, that we may repent of it and exchange it for a better. It is not right for any one to be ignorant of his own character and to go on blindfolded. We should know just what we are, what we are doing and where we are going, so that we may correct what is wrong and supply what is wanting. The best way to do this is to examine ourselves, bring ourselves to a strict account, and consider our ways.

Galatians vi. 7. Be not deceived : God is not mocked :
for whatsoever a man soweth, that shall he also reap.

IF a farmer sows a particular kind of grain, he
expects a crop of the same kind, and not of
another kind. If he sowed rye, he would be
laughed at, if he expected in the harvest, to find
that it produced a crop of wheat. Just so it is
in the moral and religious world. We may judge
from a man's present conduct what he will be
hereafter. He will reap just as he sows. Thus
for instance, if a man is too idle to work, we
may expect to find him a beggar in the end, and
perhaps dead in an alms-house. If a man becomes a drunkard, in the end he will be poor, ragged, diseased, and despised. In short, if a man
leads a wicked life, he cannot even in this life
prosper, and in the world to come, he will find
that he has lost all. If ye sow to the flesh, ye
shall of the flesh reap corruption, but if ye sow
to the Spirit, ye shall of the Spirit reap life everlasting. Every man shapes his own eternity. If
one, in spite of temptation, lives a holy life, heaven will certainly become his final dwelling place ;
but can any one reasonably suppose, that the man
who has been a profane swearer, an unclean person, a thief, a drunkard, a liar, and such like, shall
reap the rewards of religion in the other world ?
Could any one believe that the man that defied

God by his wickedness, and laughed at the Gospel of Christ, and hated religious people, and lived in the indulgence of his lusts, should at last find a place in God's presence, where the impure in heart cannot enter ? No, heaven would be a hell to such, because they are not fitted to enjoy it.   Only the pure in heart and life, can enter there, for just as a man sows so must he expect to reap.

Ecclesiastes viii. 11.   Because sentence against an evil work is not executed speedily, therefore the heart of the sons of men is fully set in them to do evil.

The man who breaks the law of his country, however he may deserve punishment, may escape by fleeing, or by bribing those who should execute the laws ; but it is not so in regard to the laws of God.   No transgressor can flee where God cannot find him, nor can any one bribe the Almighty.   And yet although his law is holy, just and good, and he will suffer no one to trample on it with impunity, yet so merciful and long-suffering is he, that he will often delay punishment for a great length of time ; sometimes for twenty years, or forty, or sixty, leaving men to grow old in sin without bringing his judgments upon them. His kind object is that sinners may be brought to repentance, and have no ground for saying that they had no time or opportunity for turning from their sins.

But see how sinners abuse this forbearance. Their heart is fully set in them to do evil, that is, they are disposed to say, God does not see us, or he does not care how we act, for we have been sinning long, and he has not punished us, and now we will go on, and sin more and more. How ungrateful is this, and how foolish too! If the sentence is not executed speedily, it will be executed at last, and the longer it is delayed the heavier it will come. A man may be sentenced to death, and be kept a year or more before he is hanged, and yet be hanged at last; and God, who has said of every sinner, that he is condemned already, may spare him even three score years and ten, but even at that age he will destroy him, if he repents not. Do not therefore abuse God's mercy, but seize this favourable time, before your day of grace is over, and turn to him with your whole heart. For Christ's sake, who died for sinners, he is willing to receive and save all who repent and believe in Jesus.

Mark vi. 48. And about the fourth watch of the night he cometh unto them, walking upon the sea, and would have passed by them.

THIS occurred on the sea of Tiberias, which is so called although it was a lake. It was subject to very fierce and sudden winds which made it dangerous. The disciples of Christ were in a boat at night rowing against a head wind, when they saw one walking on the water, and superstitiously thought it was a spirit or ghost. It was however the Son of God, and yet he was passing by them without seeming to notice them. They then cried out with fear, and immediately he encouraged them saying "Be of good cheer, it is I, be not afraid," and the wind went down and they were safe. Mariners especially are often in great danger. They are exposed to fierce winds and tempests, and the violent tossings of the ocean, and yet, so to speak, there is only a plank between them and eternity. At such times all human help may be far away and yet God Almighty is ever near, who can make the storm a calm, if they will but call upon him. But there are other dangers beside those which threaten our lives; we mean the dangers to which our souls are exposed, and these are more to be dreaded, although they do not seem so real. Now in all such dangers Christ is passing by, whether we see him or not, and he will pass by

22

unless we cry to him for help. He is able to save to the uttermost if we come to him; but he will not save, unless we feel our need of him and call upon him for mercy. He is a very present help in trouble, and why should we not apply to him? Would it not be madness in a sailor, who was in danger of drowning, to refuse to take hold of the life buoy which was thrown out to him, and which was within his reach? And will it not be greater madness in a sinner who is in danger of sinking into hell, if he refuses to take hold of Christ when he comes to him, and holds out his hand to save him? Now is the accepted time; now is the day of salvation.

Hebrews ix. 27. It is appointed unto men once to die.

YES, it is appointed unto men once to die! That is, God has fixed it as a certain rule from which there is no exception. It is the certain fate of the rich as well as the poor, the wise as well as the foolish. Death enters the gate of the palace, as well as the door of the cottage. At the call of this messenger, the farmer must leave his plow, and the sailor his ship. Death sometimes completes his work with a sudden stroke, and sometimes by a slow and painful disease; sometimes by accident on land, and sometimes by drowning at sea; sometimes in battle, and sometimes in our own houses. He has always, and in all places, the ready instruments for executing his purpose. Not only the manner of our death is appointed, but the exact time and place. It comes to some in youth, to others in mature life, and to others still in old age. When the time comes, there is no escape. Medicine cannot cure death, nor can the strong man shake it off. It is a powerful conqueror, and every hour of every day witnesses its victories. It is a foolish boast in any one to say, I am too young and hearty to die; for one stroke of death can turn strength into weakness. Thus it is appointed unto all men, without exception, to die *once*; yes, it is only once we can die here, and hence the importance of being prepared for the event. Our future condition depends on the condition in which we die. If death comes to us when we are impenitent and living in the practice of our sins, it will be, of all events, the most terrible for us; for just as death leaves us, so the judgment will find us. After death comes the judgment. Men may wickedly boast that they are not afraid of death, but that does not make it less terrible. Their boasting is turned into despair when they have to face an angry God. The true wisdom is to meet death as a friend who will introduce us into the heavenly world. This we can do by believing in Jesus who has taken away the sting of death. When we are his disciples,

and live in this world according to his commandments, we know that he will not leave us when
death comes. He will cheer us; he will safely
convey us through the dark valley, and enable us
to cry out, O death, where is thy sting? O grave,
where is thy victory?

FRIENDLY ADVICES TO SEAMEN.

THE true friend of the sailor is not one who will
lead him into dissipation, and tempt him to
do those things which will injure his health; deprive him of his hard-earned wages; destroy his
character; and endanger his soul. In every port
such pretended friends are to be found who care
not for the interests of sailors, but have their own
wicked and selfish ends to answer. Presuming on
the social and open-hearted feelings of the sailor,
and his natural desire to partake of recreation
after long voyages, they are ready to spread before
him the sensual baits which would be most likely
to captivate him. These, alas! too often prove
successful and even in opposition to better counsels. The sailor, freed from the strict discipline
of the ship and flush of money, gives loose to his
feelings, and rushes into dissipation as if it were
the chief pleasure of life. Strange and unprincipled women employ their arts to entrap him, and

houses of infamy open their doors with seeming hospitality ; and soon they are engaged in wild merriment, inflamed with liquor, and involved in fights and broils, which bring them into disgrace and difficulty, and painfully prove that the way of the transgressor is hard. Deprived of their money, these tempters at once desert them, cast them adrift, and never prove themselves to be friends in the time of need. Such being too often the experience of the too credulous sailor, we would, as their true friends, venture to give them a few friendly counsels and advices. We can have no other object than to do them good, and to warn them against practices which can only turn out to their disadvantage. Give heed then, ye generous and hardy mariners; act wisely while you have the opportunity, and be assured that you will never have cause to repent, if you now determine to follow the better course which we point out to you.

1. Then, resolve that you will give no reason to landsmen to say that you are wild, careless, and unprincipled ; that when you have money, you do not know how to take care of it ; and that when you are in port, you have no higher pleasure than a drunken frolic and a noisy brawl. Seamen should have more respect for themselves than to give occasion for such charges. Their calling is a noble and a dangerous one ; its duties are best performed by a hale, strong body and a virtuous

22 *

mind ; and nothing can so unfit them for duty as that low dissipation, which soon breaks down both body and mind. In order to this,

2. While you are on shipboard, be steady, sober, attentive to duty, and careful how you listen to the corrupting conversation of wicked sailors who have no regard for God or man. Keep as much as possible out of the company of those who would tempt you to be as wicked as themselves, and who, on shore, would be the first to entice you to improper places. A sailor may be as moral and respectable as any other man; and if he will exert himself, he may form as good a character as any other. This will require exertion and self-denial; but surely it is worth all the pains it may require. If sailors would rise in their profession, they must show by their conduct that they know how to govern themselves. Good seamanship, in connection with good conduct, is the sure road to promotion.

3. In immediate connection with this advice, we would earnestly recommend to every seaman, never to leave port without a few good books. There are intervals of time, brief as they may be, which may be best employed in reading; and it is astonishing how much useful information may be picked up in this way. Men have risen to distinction, who had no more time to read than mariners usually have. And how much better

to employ spare hours in this way, than in joking and "spinning yarns," as sailors call it! No sailor, who values his present and eternal welfare, should be without his Bible, and he should be too manly to be laughed out of this, by profane and thoughtless companions. A book on navigation, or one of voyages and travels, or on some other useful subject, will not be out of place. Sailors must read, or they must remain ignorant, and there is no greater bar to prospering in the world than ignorance.

4. Sailors should take care of their money. They earn it hard, and they should not squander it. They are usually thought to be the most improvident of men, and as careless in spending money as children. There is too much truth in this. We have known whole ships' companies, when paid off, to go on shore with their pockets full, and never rest until they had most foolishly squandered the whole, leaving themselves without enough to buy necessary clothing. Not only is the money gone, but spent in the indulgence of vices which degrade them, and ruin their health. Now we would give you a friend's advice, that instead of acting in this way, you should be saving. If you have families, remember them. If you have neither wife nor children, you may have a father, mother, or sister, who would be glad of your aid. What you have, after necessary ex-

penses, put into some safe SAVING FUND, where it will accumulate, and thus lay by something for a time of sickness, or when you shall be past service. This is much better than to depend on the charity of others, or go to a hospital, and it is much more manly. Avoid extravagance, throw not away your money in frolicking, but make provision for a future day.

5. When you arrive in port, if you have not your own houses to go to, seek out a respectable place of boarding, and especially some well conducted *Sailor's Home*, which may be found in some of the principal ports. Stand aloof from those " land sharks" who will be ready to invite you to some low boarding house, that they may clean out your pockets and then send you adrift; or get you into debt, and then ship you, taking your advance pay and leaving you nothing to provide necessaries for your voyage. These men are your greatest enemies, and the less you have to do with them, the better will it be for yourselves. And suffer not yourselves to be ensnared by profligate women, the very offscouring of the earth, who will plunder you of all you have, and injure you both in soul and body. In every port you will find such people, who, under pretence of taking an interest in you, will do you all the mischief they can. BEWARE OF THEM, and again we say, BEWARE OF THEM.

6. Take care how you spend your Sundays in
port. " Remember the Sabbath day to keep it
holy," is God's command, and you will never prosper if you do not obey it. If there is a Mariner's
Church, or a Bethel Flag Ship where there is
preaching, you cannot spend the day better than by
attending them, and you may find friends there who
will give you good advice. If there is no church,
as it may be in foreign lands, where you cannot
understand the language, employ your time with
the Bible or some good book. Sailors suffer much,
because they have to pass so many Sundays without religious instruction. If you wish to prosper
and keep out of the way of temptation, you must
pass these holy days in as moral and religious a
manner as possible.

7. Be always respectful and obedient to your
officers, and never give ear to insubordinate men,
who may strive to sour your minds against them,
and annoy them as much as possible. There are
almost always some bad men in every ship, who
hate discipline, and who would, if they could, work
others up to the point of mutiny. Keep aloof
from such, and never listen to their bad counsels.
If you should unfortunately sail with officers who
are cross-tempered and hard upon the men, it is
far better to submit than to resist. And if your
conduct is uniformly good, you will probably find
that even such men will treat you kindly. It is

generally the case, we suppose, that bad sailors make the officers unreasonable ; and from the experience they have had in this way, they are apt to come to the conclusion that all sailors are bad, and must be treated with severity. Show such, by your good conduct, that they are mistaken, and they will soon learn to make a difference.

8. And now, in the last place, endeavour always to act from a religious principle. You are not only accountable to your officers, but to your God. His eye is upon you, and if you fear and serve him aright, there will be no danger that you will fail in your duties as seamen. Sailors may be religious, and they should be religious. Exposed as they are to so many dangers, there is a peculiar need in their case for the directions and hopes and consolations of true religion. Seek God, and he will not forsake you. You have seen how many sorrows irreligious seamen bring upon themselves. You have, no doubt, known many who have degraded themselves by their vices, and even in the prime of their manhood have brought themselves down to dishonoured graves. Their fate should be a warning to you. Religion is your best safeguard. If you have this, and act up to its principles at all times, you will best promote your own comfort and success ; you may be the means of doing much good to your shipmates, and you may even be the means of carrying the gospel to foreign

ports, by distributing good tracts and Bibles, as well as by your conversation.

And now, friends, we leave with you this book of devotion and friendly counsels, from a sincere and hearty desire to do you good; praying that Almighty God would so bless it to your souls, that you may not only enjoy the peace of God in this world, but may at last, when the voyage of life is over, enter into the port of heaven, where you will find a hearty welcome and a happy home.

THE END.

CPSIA information can be obtained
at www.ICGtesting.com
Printed in the USA
LVOW13s1448210217
524952LV00009B/776/P

9 780243 254880